FOUNDED ON IRON

THAMES IRONWORKS
AND THE ORIGINS OF
WEST HAM UNITED

FOUNDED ON IRON
THAMES IRONWORKS
AND THE ORIGINS OF
WEST HAM UNITED

BRIAN BELTON

First published in 2003 by Tempus Publishing
Reprinted 2004

Reprinted in 2010 by
The History Press
The Mill, Brimscombe Port,
Stroud, Gloucestershire, GL5 2QG
www.thehistorypress.co.uk

British Library Cataloguing in Publication Data.
A catalogue record for this book is available from the British Library.

ISBN 978 0 7524 2928 1

Typesetting and origination by Tempus Publishing Limited
Printed and bound in Great Britain

Contents

Foreword by Glenn Roeder

I have been a West Ham supporter since I was a boy – coming from the area around the club, this was only natural. Most people with only a passing interest in the Hammers know that the team's badge, with its crossed 'irons', harks back to the days of Thames Ironworks Football Club, the works side that was attached to one of the biggest shipyards in the country. This was the team that would one day become West Ham United and move from the Memorial Ground to Upton Park, win the game's oldest and proudest trophy, conquer Europe, find a skipper that would rule the world and play in the most exciting and powerful league on earth.

However, more importantly, over the generations West Ham United has captured the hearts, minds and souls of millions of East Enders and honorary cockneys in places as far apart as Norway and Australia, Hong Kong and Ireland, the USA and South Africa. As such, West Ham represents a heritage of sentiment, fortitude and the type of loyalty synonymous with the communities that have lived, worked and, at times, fought and died, around London's docklands.

In *Founded on Iron,* Brian Belton has looked back to the first days of football in the part of Britain's capital that was to be associated with claret and blue. Anyone who has loved West Ham should turn these pages, as should those who want to understand the nature and personality of the people who have supported the club for over a century.

Introduction

Canning Town and West Ham, generally in those days even, was a hotbed of football…when the Thames Ironworks F.C. came before the local public a great deal was known about the game: and indeed, the way had been prepared for the Ironworks by clubs like St Lukes, Old St Lukes, and Old Castle Swifts.
                                   Syd King (1906) in *The Book of Football*

This book looks at the development of an exceptional football team, West Ham United, from its very first days – the days before they were Hammers. It charts how the 'Irons', the Thames Ironworks Football Club, were born in the docklands of London's East End in the latter part of the industrial revolution.

West Ham are exceptional for more reasons than just occupying the lower reaches of the Premiership. They, more than any other team in England, have reflected the character and atmosphere of the community from which they sprang and evolved. It is likely that more words have been written about West Ham United than any other football team of their size and standard. This is perhaps because they maintain a close affiliation with a part of London that has continued to fascinate academics, be they sociologists, anthropologists, criminologists or literary artists from a range of written genre, starting well before Jack London carried his pen east of the Tower. The area has, over the years, also been of constant interest to television in the shape of soap opera and documentary. The cinema has also had a continuing fascination with 'cockney types', from *Brighton Rock* to *Lock, Stock*; Ronnie and Reggie Kray to *The Long Good Friday*.

The Thames Ironworks was more than a football club. The team grew out of the strange combination of philanthropy and class conflict that moulded industrial relations at the end of the nineteenth century. It was the product of the people of West Ham and Canning Town in a strained collusion with the patronage of a massive, primal, capitalist employer – large even on a national scale. Thames Ironworks was the culmination of generations of industrial enterprise on the part of one phenomenal family that combined massive energy with industrial brilliance, a huge understanding of the chemical science of the Victorian period and entrepreneurial genius.

As much as anything else, *Founded on Iron* records this combined enterprise and its contribution to the development of a great swath of the capital city of the most colossal and powerful empire the world had ever seen. These were Victorians with attitude. They had extraordinary drive and a deep, heartfelt passion that probably died with that era. To understand that time, we need to try to comprehend them and their ilk. What follows is a tribute to them, the original Irons and homage to the lineage of all the Hammers to come.

—୬ One ୬—

The First Season
1895/96

On September 7, 1895, eleven men from the works turned out at Hermit Road to play the reserve team of the Royal Ordnance F.C. The pages of history record that the result was a draw, 1-1, and everybody went home satisfied. The Ironworks' first season came to a close, with happy results.

Syd King (1906) in *The Book of Football*

Towards the end of the nineteenth century, the Thames Ironworks and Shipbuilding Company Limited was one of the biggest and most important shipbuilders in Britain. At the height of its activity, the Thames Ironworks yards had eight slipways grouped in the two locations. The three lower slips faced almost due south down Bow Creek, at Canning Town, while the five upper slips lay at a north–west to south-east angle further upstream.

Soon Orchard Yard, situated just across the river to where the Millennium Dome would squat like a dying crab over a hundred and fifty years later, was beginning to ring, almost non-stop, with the sound of a gigantic orchestra of riveting hammers. It took the expertise of more than a score of trades to give shape and form to a ship, but it was the riveters binding the great iron hulls of Victorian maritime supremacy together in the dark, hard womb of the yards who were always regarded as the backbone of the shipyard. Come torrential rain, steely cold or stifling heat, they laboured, machine-like, in units of five.

It would be the role of the apprentice to bring the hundredweight sack of 200 panhead rivets, that might have to have been heaved up as high as eight or nine dozen feet to a work station, from the rivet heater or 'rivet-boy' as they were generally known, even if this person was well advanced in years. When the rivets finally got to the site of their intended use they were placed over coals in shallow pans that would also be used to heat up a brew when required. With the energetic pumping of bellows, the rivets, like malicious fireflies, would glow white-hot. At this point the molten bolts were passed with long tongs to the 'catch-boy' or 'putter-in' who would, with smaller tongs, put the reddening pins into holes previously driven in the steel plate. No sooner had the rivet reached its designated place than the 'holder-on' would wield a sixteen-pound sledgehammer with sweet accuracy to flatten the head of the nail. When the rivet had been smashed home as hard as possible, the holder-on would press on the head of the rivet with his hammerhead.

The catch-boys and the holder-on operated inside the hull, whilst the riveters laboured on the outside, braving the cruelties of the weather. Two riveters, one left-handed, another right-handed, would wait on the toil of the holder-on. Their weapon of work was a more subtle foil – a species of mallet, with a relatively slim, elongated head. These sleek but powerful riveting hammers would one day symbolise football in East London and become a distinctive element of the club crest to be worn on the heart of every player to take the field in the cause of West Ham United down the generations. These hammers were swung with unfailing precision to conclude the riveting process, that merely signalled the start of a repeat performance of the whole sequence, thousands and thousands of times until the trussing of iron to iron had melded another gargantuan hull, destined to enter into life through the birth canal of the Lea.

Many hundreds of riveting teams worked side by side in the industrious yards that blistered from every estuary, brook and creek along the eastern Thames at the end of the nineteenth century. As the rest of London town quietened as evening drew on, the 'tink' and 'tank' of these men's toil, at Canning Town, Blackwall and Limehouse, combined with an unremitting industrial percussion beating forth in a brooding bass thunder from the Millwall Ironworks, rolling out steel, and the satanic rhythm of the huge steam hammers that banged and thumped on what seemed like each spit, reach and wharf. This chaotic timbre would, in strange collisions of place and time, achieve a harmony with the hoots, toots and bellows of the collective horns of the plethora of craft that bustled on the watery highway of the Thames.

When the early darkness shrouded the metropolis in the grey metallic winter, this devils' chorus was illuminated by a cavalcade of 'firefalls', hot fragments of metal showering in sheets that flowed down the shear face of mighty hulls, skipped over bulkheads and 'drenched' decks. This incandescence would have been reiterated in reflection by the pitch mirror of water, and was the product of a thousand burners knitting iron and steel (welding didn't come to shipyards until 1940) ignited and fanned by regiments of the charred imps who were employed to stoke the collective inferno of the yards. Rivet fires punctuated the prospect like smouldering lava pools.

On 29 June 1895, the *Thames Ironworks Gazette*, the company newspaper, told its readers that:

Mr Taylor, who is working in the Shipbuilding Department, has undertaken to get up a Football Club for next winter and I learn that quoits and bowls will also be added to the attractions of the Hermit Road ground...

Dave Taylor, who was a foreman in the shipbuilding yard and also a local football referee, spent the summer of 1895 planning the new club's first season. Workers were invited to join the club for a membership fee of half a crown. This was equivalent to about 30 per cent of a riveter's weekly pay. It was planned that the side would practise and play matches at the nearby park area, in Hermit Road, Canning Town, which had be used for other sports activities organised within the company. Membership subscriptions would help finance the new club, although it was accepted that in the first instance much of the money needed to run the team would come directly from the coffers of Arnold Hills, the owner of the Thames Ironworks.

Initially Taylor was looking to organise four teams, but when just fifty applications for membership were received it was clear that this number could not adequately supply personnel for more than two teams. Taylor accordingly arranged fixtures and affiliated the Thames Ironworks Football Club to the Football Association. He also entered both sides in local cup competitions and arranged friendly matches.

At first Thames did not join a league. It is not known if this was a conscious decision, but Thames' first timetable of matches was much closer to the schedule of a professional club than that of a typical works team. It included matches against one First Division team and two clubs from the Southern League.

With Thames now ready for their first season of football, Dave Taylor stood down from his position to concentrate on refereeing and was replaced by A.T. ('Ted') Harsent, another Thames Ironworks employee who lived close to the Works in Mary Street, Canning Town. Harsent became the first secretary of Thames Ironworks Football Club. Francis Payne was the chair of the new club; he worked as a company secretary in the Ironworks. Payne was involved in several of the other works associations, most notably as vice president of the Temperance League. The existence of this particular group, alongside Arnold Hills' personal commitment to alcoholic abstinence, might go some way to explaining why the first Ironworks teams were teetotal and also non-smokers. Five years later, when Thames Ironworks FC had become West Ham United, the *East Ham Echo* still referred to the team as 'The Teetotallers'.

From the very beginning of their history, Thames were an ambitious side. Not content with testing themselves against local amateur teams, the club entered the FA Cup. This represented a relatively swift recognition by the tsars of late Victorian football and was probably facilitated through the influence and connections of Arnold Hills. The club secretary told of his side's conviction and reasoning: 'Having some good men in the club, we somewhat presumptuously considered it would be wise to enter the English Association Cup.'

Thames would have had no realistic chance of winning the competition, but participation would test the team's ability, add to the status of the new club and provide publicity. If they were lucky enough to be drawn against a good professional side, this would also considerably bolster their funds.

Thames played their first match on Saturday 7 September 1895. The game was played on their Hermit Road home ground, known locally as the 'Cinder Heap'. This location had previously been the home to Old Castle Swifts. Thames took over the tenancy when the Swifts dissolved into the annals of East London football. Royal Ordnance were the visitors that late autumn day. They were what might today be known as a 'nursery club' for Woolwich Arsenal. There is no record of the names of the Thames XI that took the field for this football baptism, but there must have been a fair number of players who were employed at the Ironworks if Syd King's recollections were accurate. In 1906 the former Thames player and West Ham manager from 1902 to 1932, explained the early formation of club policy in *The Book of Football*:

In the summer of 1895, when the clanging of 'hammers' was heard on the banks of Father Thames and the great warships were rearing their heads above the Victoria Dock Road, a few enthusiasts, with the love of football within them, were talking about the grand old game and the formation of a club for the workers of Thames Ironworks Limited.

There were platers and riveters in the Limited who had chased the big ball in the north country. There were men among them who had learned to give the subtle pass and to urge the leather goalwards.

No thought of professionalism, I may say, was ever contemplated by the founders. They meant to run their club on amateur lines and their first principle was to choose their team from men in the works.

This lyrical homily was typical of King. It can be understood as an early example of how West Ham United have been portrayed down the years. Descriptions of the club's traditions – which have been referred to, with almost Zen-like overtones, 'The West Ham Way' – have been framed in a form of romanticism. This has usually been coupled with attempts to emphasise respectability and the club's apparent mission to produce a brand of football aesthetic. Upton Park has been vaulted as a Camelot of soccer chivalry, with an Arthurian manager ruling 'the Academy' according to 'standards', 'values' and 'principles' of football purity. There is a message here that says something like: We might not win as many games as other teams, but that's because we play to an ethic. We are above winning for winning's sake and so never fail to leave the field victorious.

As will be seen, this 'holier than thou' attitude may reflect the origins of the club and the moral foundations of its existence. However, what has become a 'culture of excuse' may have done much to hold the team back in the field of modern competition.

The Iron Workers acquitted themselves well in their first outing, pulling off a commendable 1-1 draw against experienced opposition.

Following their first official match, the *Kentish Mercury* correspondent observed that not a few Thames players had been with other East London clubs the previous season. These were the 'good men' referred to by the secretary and were indeed mainly recruited from leading local clubs including Anchor and Old Castle Swifts. The latter was a company club sponsored by the Castle Shipping Line. They were reputed to be the first professional club in Essex, but folded as Thames Ironworks FC came into being. Thames also won players from the parish side St Luke's, which, like the Ironworks team, took on players that had formally turned out for the Swifts, creating a kind of informal merger between the two former rivals.

J. Lindsay was probably among those who played against Royal Ordnance. He was an inside-forward and one of the players recruited from Old Castle Swifts. Lindsay played in a number of early games for the Thames. Winger G. Sage was also likely to have taken the field for that historic opening encounter. Like Lindsay, he joined Thames after the break-up of the Swifts. Sage was to turn out for the Ironworks side in their first tie in the FA Cup against Chatham and the floodlit friendly against Old St Stephens ten days before Christmas in 1895. Another probable member of the first Thames side would have been John Thomas Archer Wood, who, as might be expected of a man bearing a name with as many facets as his, also played cricket, for Essex. He was a cousin of the champion jockey Fred Archer – a more concise moniker befitting one who carries his saddle in the 'Sport of Kings'.

From their earliest days, Thames were quick to attract talent from outside their immediate catchment area. The *Kentish Mail* and *Greenwich and Deptford Observer* on 20 September 1895 noted that 'Robert Stevenson the late captain of the Arsenal team is coming from Scotland to play for the Thames Ironworks.' Syd King recalled the coming of the mighty 'Bob' in *The Book of Football*:

'Bob' Stevenson, who captained Woolwich Arsenal at one period of their existence, was the first captain of the T.I.W.

Stevenson was yet another former Swifts man to join Thames. Able to fill a full-back role or any of the three half-back positions with equal effectiveness, Bob would, at a push, also play centre-forward for Thames. He was the first player of real note to wear a Thames shirt, having previously been the skipper of Woolwich Arsenal. Born at Barrhead, Glasgow in 1869, Bob joined the Swifts from the Gunners in March 1895, but returned to Scotland following the break-up of the club. However, he was brought to Hermit Road for Thames' initial campaign and was promptly installed as club captain and assistant trainer, working alongside the forty-two-year-old guru of East London football (the Malcolm Allison of his day) Tom Robinson.

Bob moved back to his Caledonian roots after his time with the Irons, joining Arthurlie. His decision to return to Scotland for a second time was recorded in *Association Football and the Men Who Made It* by Dickford and Gibson (1905):

Robert Stevenson, a full-back of merit who captained the Arsenal team in their early Second Division struggles, was among those who helped to build warships when the suggestion of a football club was made at the Thames Ironworks, and he was the first captain of the team.

There was not much of him in the way of physique, but he was a wonderfully good player and invaluable as an advisor to the fathers of the club.

He remained with Thames Ironworks until the second season, when they were located at Browning Road, East Ham. About halfway through their campaign at this enclosure, Stevenson returned home to Scotland and played for Arthurlie.

Stevenson's alliance with trainer Tom Robinson represented something of a dream team. Robinson was another seminal figure remembered by Syd King in *The Book of Football*:

Their trainer was 'Tommy' Robinson, and he is still trainer to West Ham United. There is a break of several seasons in his service, however, during which we saw him smoking his cigar on match days and thinking hard when the game was going against the side in which he has always taken a deep interest.

Robinson was well respected in East London, having previously worked with both St Luke's and the Castle Swifts in the 1880s. Robinson, distinguishable by his huge moustache and trademark cigar, also worked with East End cyclists and boxers. He convened his training sessions in a room in Trinity Church School, Barking Road, in the recognisable trainer's attire of roll-neck woollen jumper and cloth cap. Robinson could be regularly spotted marshalling training along Turnpike Road (now Beckton Road). These sessions were evidently early morning or late evening jaunts, starting out from the club's 'indoor facility' as Syd King's recollection in *The Book of Football* indicates:

...and in those early days the training was done on week nights at a school-room in the Barking Road...The players used also to occasionally go out for a moonlight spin on the turnpike road.

This, in itself, became something of a spectacle, attracting, at times, hundreds of onlookers. The sight must have been intriguing at the time – young men, sporting woolly hats or flat caps, sometimes both, hopping, bunny jumping, skipping and piggybacking in big boots with socks pulled over trousers to the knee. Up and down the grimy dock road they would trundle, with serious, pained expressions of concentration locked on their faces, in a kind of parade that must have amused, amazed and puzzled locals – maybe even frightening a few younger ones.

The second game, against Dartford 'A', brought Thames their first victory, the *Thames Irons Works Gazette* commenting that the Kent side were given 'a licking of 4 to nil'.

Results continued to improve and on 28 September the Thames played their first away game, taking on Manor Park. It was a runaway 8-0 victory. However, all too often in their first season Thames found themselves involved in games like this, playing against sides that did not have the ability to stretch them. The team committee was looking forward to sterner, more rewarding tests and so continued to strengthen the playing squad.

The first real challenge and truly competitive match for the club came in October when they made their debut in the FA Cup. Their opponents were Chatham, a Southern League side with a growing tradition. Thames had been drawn at home, but conceded this advantage, consenting to the tie being played at Chatham following, it was said, the Kent club's request, due to the 'unsuitability' of the Hermit Road ground. Of course, the prospect of better gate receipts might also have been an unforeseen but welcome consequence for both clubs. Thames managed to compete well in the first half, but during the second period they were overrun and the game ended in a 5-0 victory for Chatham. *The Sportsman* noted that the 'goalkeeping and defence of the visitors was the best part of their play'.

Aside from the result, this first FA Cup adventure had been a resounding success: the club had earned extra revenue as a result of switching the tie to Chatham and the game had helped raise the profile of the Thames Ironworks Football Club.

By November, the committee's efforts to improve the team was paying dividends. Thames took on Southern League side Reading, considered to be one of the South's top club sides, and although they lost 3-2, the Londoners emerged with credit after dominating much of the game. This excellent display was followed by more impressive results during the winter of 1895/96, including a victory over St Luke's, who were still a potent force in the East End. After these performances, it was widely speculated that the Thames would be elevated to the Southern League for the 1896/97 term.

Let there be light

During this first season Thames attracted much interest and a certain amount of notoriety through their experimentation with floodlighting. The lighting engineers from the Ironworks were given permission to provide 'electric illumination' so that kick-off times could be moved into the late afternoons and early evenings. This would allow men from the works to attend games played during the week. The first game to enjoy this rudimentary floodlighting was a friendly against Old St Stephen's at Hermit Road on 16 December 1895. The fact that the game was refereed by Lt W. Simpson, who was to take charge of that season's FA Cup final (Sheffield Wednesday v. Wolves), underlined the status of the match. Twelve lights, each of 2,000 candlepower, were mounted on poles. The result was far from perfect. The precarious supports for the lights posed a constant threat to players and spectators alike. A Christmas tree effect was probably the best that could have been hoped for, with bulbs strung around the edge of the pitch. This was not wholly conducive to flowing football; the huge lamps blew at random intervals and had to be replaced as the game continued. There were also a number of periods when the pitch was plunged into total darkness due to a collective failure of the lighting system. One reporter commented that he heard members of the Old St Stephen's team complaining that, '...the lights always went out just when the Thames Ironworks men had a shot at goal.'

The lights were gradually improved – although throughout games the play had to be halted as the ball had to be dipped in whitewash to make it visible. However, all this effort was not unappreciated. At the end of January a report of a friendly against Barking Woodville in *The Sportsman* noted that:

...the company (Thames Ironworks) *have spared no expense,*

and that

...the light gave a good view.

Technology must have been improving by trial and error, if not injury and fatality.

In March 1896 Hermit Road played host to Woolwich Arsenal and West Bromwich Albion from the First Division of the Football League. Albion fielded the legendary Billy Basset. Thames were beaten by both big clubs, 5-3 by the Gunners and 4-2 at the hands of Basset and his Baggies, but results were very much a secondary consideration in terms of these matches. They were much more about getting Thames Ironworks Football noticed and recognised as a footballing force in East London than an end in themselves.

By the end of 1895/96, Thames were a match for any amateur side. The overall record for that first season stood at: played 46, won 30, lost 12. The Hermit Road team had scored 136 goals, conceding only 68 in the process. Secretary Harsent told the *Thames Ironworks Gazette* that this was 'a record to be proud of'.

Thames had rounded off their inaugural season by winning the West Ham Charity Cup, their first ever trophy. Thames beat Park Grove 1-0 in the semi-final at Plaistow, but following protests about a technicality from Park the tie had to be replayed. Thames went through to the final as 3-0 winners at Beckton Road.

It took three games to decide the destination of the Cup that year. Following a 2-2 draw with Barking at the Old Spotted Dog ground at Upton Lane, Forest Gate, the replay at the same venue ended in another draw, this time 0-0. In the second replay, Thames went away 2-1 winners before a crowd of more than 3,000. Thames, who were now widely known as the Irons – a reference to the hammers used to rivet ships together in the Ironworks Yard, which was just a short walk from the team's Hermit Road home – clearly needed to find regular, demanding competitive football for the 1896/97 season. The side needed something more than what had been provided thus far by the Charity Cup and Essex and London Junior Cups. Before the kick-off of the 1896/97 season, the *Thames Ironworks Gazette* announced:

With reference to the forthcoming season, it has been decided to enter for the English Cup, London Senior Cup, West Ham Charity Cup, South Essex League senior and junior and, if possible, one or two others. There will be very few dates left open for 'friendly' matches, so it ought to be a good thing for the club financially.

The Irons were, quite literally, meaning business.

—&⁊ *Two* ⁊&—

All Things Bright and Beautiful

These early organisers, of what, in a later age, is known as West Ham United, also found a generous patron in Mr A.F. Hills.

Syd King (1906) in *The Book of Football*

Frank Clarke Hills, the first of the Hills family to own the Thames Ironworks, died in May 1895. He had always been determined that one of his three sons would inherit the company and in the last years of the nineteenth century Arnold Frank Hills, who in the early 1890s had joined the board of directors of his father's shipbuilding business (the last surviving major shipbuilding company in London) after completing his education at Harrow and University College, Oxford, took over the leadership of the firm.

From the start of his career Arnold Hills showed a strong interest in the living conditions of the company workforce. At the age of twenty-three, like other young industrialists of the time working in the East London area, he decided to take a house near to his place of business. For five years he owned a small property in Canning Town, on the East India Dock Road, just a short walk from the Ironworks.

In his younger days Arnold had been a successful footballer, representing Oxford University in the Varsity match. This fixture at that time was equivalent in terms of talent and status to a top European club match today. Arnold went on to don the colours of Old Harrovians, one of England's most powerful sides in that era, and won an international cap, playing for the England team that defeated Scotland 5-4 at Kennington Oval in 1879. The young Hills was not content to restrict his sporting achievements to the confines of association football, however; he was also a star of the athletics field, gaining the coveted blue ribbon of the track when he became the English mile champion.

The rich man in his castle

In January 1895 Arnold Hills, now the owner of Thames Ironworks, began to publish his *Thames Ironworks Gazette*. This periodical was a combination of technical journal, propaganda instrument, company newsletter, popular history magazine and local newspaper, but Hills saw it as primarily providing a channel of communication between the workers and the management of his company, that would address resentment and bad feelings following the industrial strife that troubled the London docks during the latter part of the nineteenth century. Much of this antipathy had its root in Hills' decision to take on 'black' labour – casual workers, not usually employed by the Ironworks – during the withdrawal of labour. As he stated in the *Thames Ironworks Gazette* of June 1895, he wished to create:

...a fresh link of interest and fellowship between all sorts and conditions of workers in our great industrial community.

From the start the *Thames Ironworks Gazette* was Hills' mouthpiece, a potential direct line to his employees, through which he was able to advance his own world view – including the idea that the common interests of all those involved with Thames Ironworks were intrinsically tied to the prosperity of the company. Under the headline, 'The Importance of Co-operation between Workers and Management', he wrote:

But thank God this midsummer madness is passed and gone; inequities and anomalies have been done away with and now, under the Good Fellowship system and the Profit Sharing Scheme, every worker knows that his individual and social rights are absolutely secured.

This illustrates that the publication was used to inform employees about and promote support for changes in company policy that Hills had initiated, one of which was the co-ownership scheme mentioned above and another being the introduction of the first recorded eight-hour working day for his employees in 1894.

The *Thames Ironworks Gazette* also advertised corporate facilities, such as the range of worker associations and clubs that Hills had set up within his organisation. In the evenings he would often visit these societies, which included cricket, rowing, athletics and cycling clubs, a science society and a drama group. Hills saw music as being particularly important, so drawing on members of the Thames Ironworks temperance society a Temperance choir was generated. This existed together with an operatic group, a string orchestra, a military band and a brass band. The latter would play at the home matches of Thames Ironworks FC. As well as promoting these 'extra-curricular' activities, the *Thames Ironworks Gazette* kept workers informed about the progress of the various clubs, providing a results service and reporting on performances and events.

The *Thames Ironworks Gazette* appeared for over twenty years, until Hills was paralysed by arthritis. Its lead article was almost always written by Hills and often took the form of a kind of sermon, focusing on issues that attracted his interest. Invariably a political point assailed the reader, but this was not always overt and sometimes got lost in a diatribe held together by Hills' class perspective and somewhat puritan values. Couched in the contradictory blend of Christian capitalist aestheticism that was the moral engine of the Victorian elite and the bedrock on which the British Empire was built, these writings suggest that the author was a complex and driven soul. However, they also provide a clear understanding of the role of clubs and associations, alongside initiatives like the co-ownership scheme and the eight-hour day, within Thames Ironworks. They embodied the connection that Hills saw between social welfare and the development of his organisation as an effective business enterprise. This gave these groups a complex character. Hills set up the societies ostensibly to create a feeling of commonality across wage and status boundaries. This part of the plan aimed to encourage loyalty to the company, in particular amongst his shop floor employees. Out of this, Hills looked to generate a psychological fusion between everybody involved in the company that would create solidarity and a shared interest in the company's aims that were mostly defined by him. In short, Hills wanted those who sold their labour to the Ironworks for a wage to see this as a good investment, in spite of the fact that the Hills' shipyard, like all companies within the Victorian business environment, primarily existed in order that its owners might make profits by paying workers less than the true value of their labour.

This strategy was complimented by the potential of the clubs to offer an alternative form of fraternity to that found outside the company in the growing Union movement that, by making inroads on the profit margin of companies, through pressure for higher wages and better conditions, was seen by late Victorian entrepreneurs as a huge threat. To this end, Hills set up a central council to co-ordinate the efforts of the many new associations. He urged that every club should:

...rally loyally around the Central Council...and thus united...the social movement which has already done so much will go from success to success...It will set the seal upon the business prosperity of the firm and crown the labours of the Works with the laurels of the road, the river, the racing track, the field and the public hall.

Hills definitely wanted his clubs to be good at whatever they were doing, but he insisted that the council encourage the development of these societies as separate entities. This demonstrates a somewhat contradictory attitude, typical of the time – the creation of a nexus of co-operation whilst promoting competition within the same. This is not to say that Hills consciously developed this situation, but the 'house' system within public schools and the allegiance to 'college' within the university system prepared upper-class young men well for their destiny – the organisation and maintenance of Victorian society and its values. As such, the clubs were much more than merely a diversion for the participants.

Hills was not the first capitalist in the London area to seek to ingratiate himself with his workers using company benefits and the carrot of better employment conditions. When the workers of the South Metropolitan Gas Company 'left work' in 1889 (strikes were illegal at that time) in protest against the company's profit-sharing plans, owner George Livesey extended the scheme, making a huge investment in social facilities. Opposite the present Port Greenwich/ English Partnership offices stood the company's institute and theatre: both were built as part of a co-partnership initiative. This extended to a scheme that provided children born to employees with work, housing and burial at the expense of the company.

As will be seen later, the Hills family had a close association with the gas industry and were always quick to learn and benefit from it – Arnold, in this respect, was carrying on a tradition. He was a man of his era and true to the tactics of his class, but he was also part of a group of industrialists ahead of their time. Not until the 1960s did the majority of large-scale organisations in the USA and later Japan begin to rediscover the full business benefits in developing paternalistic and philanthropic relationships between themselves and their employees.

All this should not undermine the fact that Hills was certainly passionate and sincere in his hope that the worker associations and other company initiatives would positively effect worker morale and foster employment satisfaction within the Ironworks. His initiatives were not straightforward, cynical efforts to exploit his workers. His beliefs, aesthetic outlook and moral convictions, including a wish to 'better' those in his employ and his faith in the enterprise of Thames Ironworks as a philanthropic community, were deeply set. He was a man steeped in the Protestant work ethic. The making of money was considered a vulgar enterprise for a gentleman, although, in contradiction to this outlook, to be a respectable member of upper class society one certainly needed to command appreciable financial resources. The wealthy individual could ameliorate this quandary by using his wealth for a greater end and developing a sense of their 'class duties'. This was the engine of Victorian philanthropy founded on 'good works'. It became a belief system within sections of the rising industrial class of the time that gave an ethical justification for the barbarity of late nineteenth-century industrial exploitation, which functioned to make one family rich on the product of the many who laboured on the precipice of poverty. As such, Hills genuinely wanted to improve the moral and physical condition of those he relied on to keep his company profitable. This evoked in him the paternalism so typical of the time. Hills saw it as his social and religious duty as well as his personal and class responsibility to influence and if necessary finance the direction of his workers' leisure and the lives of others. As far as Hills was concerned, God had ordained his wealth and position. With this blessing came the responsibility for those in his employ.

At the 1895 meeting of the Vegetarian Federal Union Hills, as the first Chair of the Union, gave an 'inspiring' hour-long talk on vegetarianism and its benefits. On a subsequent visit to Birmingham he called together a group of businessmen and said:

I would like to see a first-class vegetarian restaurant in Birmingham and if you will start it I will subscribe ten per cent of the cost.

This was part of his personal crusade, alongside his militant advocacy of temperance, to 'purify' the world. It also demonstrates his belief in championing good causes, within a strategy of social engineering. Thus it can be understood why Hills wanted to provide his workforce with opportunities to enjoy wholesome leisure pursuits. He hoped that they would be edifying in themselves, but the clubs and societies were put in place, in the main, to divert those under his stewardship away from spending their spare time on what Hills saw as the evils of drink and gambling and provide an alternative fraternity to the pub and the union.

Hills was also, at times, to show commendable loyalty to his workforce. He would not, for instance, entertain the idea of moving his shipyards further down the Thames. This would have been more efficient, allowing for greater margins of profit, but at the same time it would have caused tremendous hardship in the area of Essex that was part of the extended East End of London and included the borough of West Ham. He also allowed Trade Union activity, even if he set up schemes looking to offer alternative forms of welfare and social activity.

By 1895 the Thames Ironworks and Ship Building Company was the largest shipbuilding yard, and certainly one of Britain's most important. The Ironworks had employed 6,000 men in 1860 and in 1890, during the great industrial action in docks, 7,000 of its men 'left work'. The docks were an important source of employment. The Victoria and Albert Docks were the largest single source of employment for men in West Ham. A great deal of cheap housing was built in the Canning Town Tidal Basin and Custom House areas of West Ham for this casual labour force that, for the sake of efficiency, needed to live close to their work. Although more than 7,000 men worked on the docks in 1904, factory work provided employment for three times as many people in West Ham. A few industrial concerns, like the Thames Ironworks, were associated with the docks, but the majority of West Ham's working population was not composed primarily of either casual labourers or dockers. The largest employers of skilled labour were the repair shops of the Great Eastern Railway. By 1904 there were more than 11,000 men working in the metal and machine trades in West Ham.

In governmental terms, West Ham was not part of London. It was an Essex suburb – a manufacturing centre, containing factories that had moved out from London. Many of these were 'offensive industries' producing dirt, fumes and chemical residues. The prevailing winds over London blow in an easterly direction and thus it made sense to rid the city of pollution by moving its filth-generating activities in that direction.

A survey published in the late 1880s had indicated that 60 per cent of the population of West Ham existed below the poverty line. Sickness, poverty, pollution and unemployment were rife. In the last two decades of the nineteenth century the district was seriously overcrowded: there was an average of 6.46 people per house in West Ham, while the average for England and Wales was 5.21. Pressure on housing was most severe in Canning Town, Custom House and Silvertown – the areas where the highest percentage of casual labourers lived. In Upton Park and Forest Gate, professional and business families occupied comfortable housing. The northern part of West Ham was described as a dormitory for London, and this increased as one went into the surrounding areas of East Ham, Barking and Ilford. The inner area of West Ham lacked open space and public recreation grounds. Most children and men who played football did so on the spaces between factories and industrial areas.

Howarth and Wilson's detailed 1907 survey of the social problems in West Ham contrasted its lack of open space with 'planned towns' like Bournville, where it was thought necessary to have undeveloped areas within a five-minute walk of homes. It was impossible to achieve this in West Ham, but the report made the point that a lack of open space 'is conducive neither to health nor to morals', and concluded that it 'was not surprising to have bands of young hooligans whose energies are expended in petty larcenies in the streets'. Hills often cited the lack of recreational facilities as one of the worst deprivations in the lives of West Ham residents. It is true that the borough had inherited most of London's worst problems – overcrowding, impoverishment and grime – but its rates were so low (another attraction for business) that it could not afford good sanitation and open play areas. Arnold Hills was to note that 'the perpetual difficulty of West Ham is its poverty. It is rich only in its population'.

In 1895, Hills vigorously supported a plan to bring the borough of West Ham into the county of London. He understood that becoming part of London administratively meant that West Ham could effectively be subsidised by the rest of the city to the benefit of the local community. He also grasped that this would improve the quality (in terms of both health and education) of the workforce and provide an impetus for the general business environment at the lower reaches of the Thames. This recognition of the relationship between social welfare and the vitality of business was evident throughout Hills' tenure in the East End as was his awareness of the value of loyalty to his workforce. Hills probably understood that company loyalty to the workforce could motivate reciprocation in the form of the working class/East End solidarity that existed in the West Ham area, harnessing this resource for the benefit of production. His faith was well founded. Arnold Hills was never let down by his workers. Subsequently, West Ham United Football Club has always benefited from the same cultural values of the district.

There can be little doubt that Arnold Hills had an authentic concern for his employees and the wider population of the West Ham community that huddled around the banks of the Thames and Lea, but these sentiments coexisted alongside a commitment to the structure of capitalist enterprise and the master/servant ethic. This was the ethos that permeated Victorian employment relations and the wider context of the British Empire. Indeed, the attitude that Hills and the likes of South Met Gas Company owner George Livesley displayed towards their employees was similar to the relationship that their class contemporaries, the well-meaning British colonial elite, fostered with 'the natives' of the great swaths of red that then dominated global maps. Both colonialist and industrialist regarded those they saw as being 'in their charge' as potentially troublesome children. As such, they needed to be educated, gainfully occupied and kept in conditions that, in times of labour shortages, would sustain an efficient, fit, skilled and devoted workforce, free from hunger and sickness – both of which were enemies of effective production.

The overall effect of Hills' investment in the free time of his workforce, in his ideal world, would be to raise the ethical and market reputation of his firm together with its efficiency. At the same time it would play a part in converting his workforce into respectable, decent, God-fearing and above all obedient members of society that knew and were content with their station in life, to produce wealth for the use of their social 'betters' who were the only group capable of using this in a responsible and effective manner. Little, it seems, changes.

The poor man at his gate

It is not clear how many Thames Ironworks employees took up the temperance advocated by Hills. It does appear, however, that many defiantly braved the moral perils that he saw as so threatening to his workforce, particularly in the Old Imperial Theatre in the Barking Road at the top of The Marsh (Victoria Dock Road), right on the doorstep of the Ironworks.

The Old Imperial started its life as the Royal Albert Music Hall, more widely known as Relf's, after the owner Charles Relf. Relf's was advertised in *The Stage* as, 'the handsomest and most comfortable (music hall) in East London, entirely lit by electricity'. Despite the efforts of Arnold Hills, it was a favourite haunt of many a Thames Ironworks riveter. The hall had its own built-in pub, The Town of Ayr, and at the height of Thames Ironworks' history it engaged acts 'at enormous expense'. These included Tom Costello (famous for the ditty 'At Trinity Church I Met Me Doom'), Charlie Coborn (who wowed audiences with his 'Two Lovely Black Eyes' and 'The Man that Broke the Bank at Monte Carlo'), Kate Carney (the voice behind 'Three Pots a Shilling'), Vesta Victoria (whose rendition of 'Waiting at the Church' was a national hit), Gus Elen (who had great success with 'It's a Great Big Shame') and Ella Shields, the original 'Burlington Bertie from Bow'.

The last pantomime to be staged at the Imperial, over the Christmas period of 1920, was *Aladdin*. One of the big successes of this production was a tableau, based on the famous Pears Soap advertisement and the song 'I'm Forever Blowing Bubbles'. Audiences joined in with great gusto and soon the tune was to be heard all over the East End, whistled in streets, sung in pubs, clubs and, of course, at the Boleyn ground. The funny, melancholic little tune would become synonymous with the progenitor of Thames Ironworks Football Club, West Ham United.

The question of who was to run Thames Ironworks FC was posed from the very earliest days. There was, almost from the inception of the club, a desire for independence and a level of professionalism.

This was illustrated when in 1895 the Thames players decided that the club's governing committee should be made up of non-players. The *Thames Ironworks Gazette* reported that 'a number of gentlemen were asked to fulfil this function, which proved most beneficial to the club.'

This group was made up of clerks, foremen and supervisors at the Ironworks. It would regularly find itself at loggerheads with Arnold Hills and occasionally openly rebelled against his passionate support of the virtues of sporting amateurism. This was a struggle between the committee seeking to actualise their vision for the football club and Hills' abhorrence of the growing tide of professionalism in Victorian sport. The new club had already shown its ambition by developing an active committee, recruiting top coaching and playing staff and by organising a fixture list with a distinctly professional look about it, including entry into the FA Cup. The very first foray in the Cup was telling in terms of understanding the future aims of the football club. One of the main reasons for taking part in the competition was to raise the profile of Thames Ironworks Football Club. The committee also chose to waive home advantage and that meant extra cash was raised from gate receipts. This strategy emphasised the movement the club was making towards professionalism. The game was not being played for an end in itself, as would befit the amateur code of conduct, so close to the heart of Arnold Hills.

Thus Thames Ironworks Football Club was born and the foundations of West Ham United put down. But the roots of East London football go deeper. People had been kicking balls to rules in around the fringes of the Thames docklands long before Arnold Hills had dreamt of building ships in Canning Town.

—❧ *Three* ❧—

Gentleman Footballers

I ought to point out that West Ham is one of the oldest football centres in the country. The fact is not generally known that Blackburn Rovers have met Upton Park – not the present club of that name – in a late round of the Association Cup competition in West Ham Park. 'The oldest inhabitant' tells me that Blackburn Rovers won.

Syd King (1906) in *The Book of Football*

Millwall and Woolwich Arsenal were well-established football clubs in London by the time the idea to form a football club within the Thames Ironworks had been mooted. Both Arsenal and Millwall had evolved out of works teams. However, Millwall and the Thames Ironworks Football Club were not the first competent and organised football teams to see light in the Dockland area. Football was well established in Britain before the turn of the nineteenth century. However, it was only during the 1800s that the game developed from a rough, traditional mob pursuit, without any definite restrictions of time or space, into an organised sport, defined by rules, within temporal limitations and conventions of play.

This systematised and controlled game was the product of England's public schools. The aim of this exercise was to divert young men from what were seen by their elders as sinful, corrupt and wasteful preoccupations and offer a wholesome alternative, that would encourage honour in 'sportsmanship' and 'manly' fraternity.

Wigglesworth in *The Evolution of English Sport* (1996) argued that the notion of amateurism was nurtured from the 'gentlemen' of the eighteenth century who 'dabbled nonchalantly' in the arts with no aim towards achieving excellence. They saw those with professional interests in the pursuit of the arts and the mastering of the same as crude and, as such, unworthy to hold the distinction of the title of gentleman. This attitude carried over into the realms of sport and the professional sportsman, alongside the tradesman, needed, at least, to be kept at arms length by their 'betters'. Within the public school structure, sport was employed to promote the whole system of class distinction, emphasising lines of demarcation and symbolising the fantasy of moral, cultural and even spiritual superiority.

The extension of the franchise, which caused a wider consciousness of class dissatisfaction, and the broader governmental awareness of the needs of capital (a fit, compliant, contented workforce with a basic education) led to a gradual rise in the age of school attendance and the slow reduction in the length of the working day. This gave people a new measure of free time. Many of them filled this with sport.

Alongside this, the recognition of professionalism within football, in 1885, seemed to make it more necessary for socially advantaged groups to maintain the distinction between sport as a noble, society and character-building pursuit and sport as a job of work. This was not wholly about money. The upper and higher middle classes had for hundreds of years been involved in efforts to profit financially from sport through gambling on horse racing and prize-fighting amongst other things. Nor was it connected to the possibility that payment would allow workers to become as accomplished as their class superiors, having the opportunity to train full-time.

Organised sport in general and football in particular had proved, within the public school environment, to be a useful means to explain, justify and so reinforce class hierarchy. As such, it is not surprising that a colonial culture would seek to broaden the social lessons it wanted to teach through sport, beyond the public schools. This would only be possible through the creation of a regulated form of play.

Standardisation

It was in 1863 that the newly-formed English Football Association, which was largely made up of men from public school backgrounds, planned to draft a set of rules that would be acceptable to players all over the country. They used Cambridge University rules as a template, which were, in effect, a conflation of regulations for the game drawn from the various public schools that students studying at the university had attended. These laws took some time to gain general acceptance. The Sheffield Association, for example, took until 1877 to abandon its own version of the offside rule. The resistance of some clubs to the FA's regulations at points turned into open rebellion. There was a particular dislike of directives referring to 'hacking' (kicking the shins of an opponent). Some sides used a combination of the FA rules and their own. A number of public schools like Brentwood accepted the FA laws, but many of the better-known footballing schools like Eton and Winchester retained their own conventions. The eventual split in the Association gave rise to the Rugby Football Union, but whilst the old boy teams of the public schools conformed to the FA's laws, there were times when teams played under both FA and Rugby Football Union codes in order to be able to play regular games. A former pupil from Brentwood School remembered that in the 1860s his school team was able to arrange association fixtures with St Paul's and Merchant Tailors' only when there had been an agreement to turn out against them under Rugby Football Union rules.

The growth of association football was slow at first. The majority of the new clubs were situated in and around London. Most leading players had learnt their skills at public schools or the universities. In these early years the clubs stayed true to a strict amateur code, set within 'the Corinthian spirit', the overriding consideration being focused on how the game was played.

The outstanding teams in the first twenty years of the existence of the Football Association were those of old boy clubs. The Old Etonians and Old Harrovians – the Manchester United and Arsenal of their day – were made up of players who had attended the public schools of Eton and Harrow. The Wanderers was a team made up of the past pupils of several public schools. At the eastern borders of London and Essex, Upton Park Football Club was a side of this type. It developed during the first decades of the Football Association and was the first club to make an impact on the East London, Dockland district. That Upton Park FC was born into an area that was becoming a densely populated industrial district did not make it immune from the social prejudice characteristic of its public school roots. However, Upton Park, albeit unwittingly, would play a part in bridging the gap that separated organised football from the working-class people.

Upton Park Football Club

Seven hundred ladies and gentlemen attended Upton Park Football Club's annual sports day at the end of the 1867/68 season. The local newspaper reported that such a good turn out was due to the good weather and the fact that the 'rough element' had been excluded.

How the rough element were kept out was not detailed, but it must have required a considerable security operation, as the track used for the event was merely an unenclosed section of the north-east corner of John Gurney's spacious grounds. This area was then known as Upton Park. It was soon to be transformed into a public amenity and became known (as it is now) as West Ham Park. What kind of threat the rough element posed can only be guessed. Maybe it was thought that they would look to disrupt an event organised by their betters. Perhaps the fear was that these social inferiors might have ambitions to run in the races. Traditionally, athletic and football events were relatively informal affairs, normally held in conjunction with festivals, and usually open to anyone who wished to take part in them. However, in sport as elsewhere, things were changing quickly in mid-Victorian England. The rules of athletics were sufficiently well established for the Amateur Athletic Club to hold an annual championship meeting at West Brompton. This was later to develop into the Amateur Athletic Association championships.

The events taking place at Upton Park on that sunny day in 1868 were highly formalised contests of athletic prowess. Their organisation represented the apparent gulf between the lower orders and the upper echelon of society. The competitors that day would not have been taking part in physical encounters merely for fun or financial gain. For this group of people, sport would have epitomised the cultivation of the gentlemanly character and captured the spiritual quality of what it was to be English. This ethic was exemplified when Upton Park FC objected to Preston North End's inclusion in the 1883/84 FA Cup on the grounds that players were being paid. This was to lead directly to Preston's expulsion from the competition, and the unintended consequence, from Upton Park FC's point of view, of the FA becoming more tolerant of professionalism, although under strictly monitored conditions.

There might have been confusion about rules of football elsewhere, but not at the Upton Park Football Club. Two of their players of the 1860s, C.W. Alcock and A. Stairs, had been intimately involved with the early progress of association football and had been part of the seminal discussions about the nature of the rules of the game. Stairs was to be elected as treasurer of the FA in 1871 and was later appointed as its assistant secretary. Alcock had previously been a member of the Snaresbrook-based Forest Club and went on to captain the Wanderers side that had been victorious in the 1873 FA Cup final. From 1866 he had been an influential member of the FA committee. This was also the year in which Upton Park FC was founded. Alcock had an important role in heightening the profile of association football through his reputation as a player and administrator of the game, but he was also editor of the *FA Annual*. This quasi-official journal published information about changes to rules and provided a record of games played in a season and the following season's fixtures. It also included profiles of prominent players and details of representative teams, lists of club grounds and officers. As such, football history owes a great deal to the *FA Annual* and the work of C.W. Alcock.

Upton Park FC was a regular in the FA Cup – the only national football competition that existed at the time. The team didn't get past the first round until 1875/76, being eliminated in the second round. However, the following season saw Upton Park capture national attention. An FA Cup run that included victories over Leyton, Barnes and Marlow took the team into the last rounds of the competition. Holding Oxford University, a huge side at that time, to a draw in the last six, they lost the replay 1-0. This effectively cost Upton Park a place in the final as Oxford were given a bye in the semi-final (they lost to the Wanderers in the final).

Upton Park continued to impress in the 1877/78 term. They stormed through to the fourth round of the FA Cup and were only stopped by the major footballing power, the Old Harrovians. Upton Park had moved from being a relatively unknown side to one of the strongest teams in the country. They were producing and attracting some top players. Goalkeeper C. Warner went on to gain an England cap and R.A. Ogilvie, who was to spend three seasons with Upton Park after he left Brentwood, went on to play in the 1878/79 FA Cup final with Clapham Rovers. He also gained an international cap, turning out for England against Scotland. C. Mitchell, the former captain of Felsted public school, played in many of Upton Park's great matches in the 1880s and he earned five England caps while with the club. R.S. Bastard was one of the best players to turn out for Upton Park. He had attended the City of London School before studying law. He gained one England cap during his time with Upton Park and was later given the great honour of refereeing the 1877/78 FA Cup final.

In the first years of its existence, most Upton Park players were born or lived in the area around Upton Park and as the club grew more successful it still sought to draw on resources in the local area without compromising its public school foundations. For example, local clergymen and ordinands were recruited, drawn to the area by a commitment to muscular Christianity that was a major factor in the development of the public school missions and university settlements that were being established in East London at the time. However, Upton Park's years of success were still premised on recruiting from far and wide through an old boy network. This was motivated by a desire to maintain their exclusivity, but at the same time to further the footballing ambitions of the club through the winning of matches at the highest level.

Upton Park established itself as the top London club when the side won the first London FA Cup in 1882/83. They retained the trophy the following season and went on to enjoy several more protracted runs in the FA Cup. As such, they represent the first glow of football success in the area which was to be dominated by Thames Ironworks Football Club and then West Ham United.

Half a dozen Upton Park players had been members of N.L. Jackson's exclusive Corinthian FC in the 1880s and it was that tradition that dominated Upton Park's ethos. Upton Park had absolutely no interest in cultivating the football potential in local working-class boys. For all this, the future of association football at the highest level, in East London as elsewhere, relied on working-class boys. Football's lifeblood would be the lads that kicked rags or paper tied up with string in parks, on waste ground, in the playgrounds of the new Board Schools, or in the streets and alleyways that huddled around the docks, wharves and factories. Teachers in the elementary schools, youth workers associated with the university settlement movement and the public school missions aided the development of the West Ham Schools' Football Association that was founded in 1890. Over the next thirty years it was to become one of the best school football associations in England, winning the national championship (the English Schools' Shield) on several occasions.

There were fine football teams established by the public school missions that had been set up in the area. The Malvern Mission in Canning Town that was run in association with the Church Lads' Brigade was a strong side, but it was Fairbairn House, the youth club attached to the Mansfield House Settlement in Canning Town, which was to foster much of the football ability to be found in the youth of West Ham. Many young men had their first taste of organised football in the West Ham Schools' League and went on, after leaving school, to play as youths for Fairbairn House. From there, they often went on to local junior sides or to the good amateur and professional clubs. A few, like Jack Tresadern, Syd Puddifoot and Stanley Earle – all of whom had played in the West Ham Schools' League – went on to play for West Ham United and, along with Harold Halse, England.

However, it was Upton Park FC that had started football rolling in the area. Thousands of young boys would have seen their first top quality games as spectators at Upton Park and been inspired to take up and work at the game by the exploits of these committed Corinthians. As such, Upton Park FC can be understood as the seed corn of football in East London. Part of their morality, that the game provided a means to develop character and the values requisite to the leading of a decent life, was replicated in the university settlements and missions that in turn would act as the footballing nurseries of talent in the most working class of districts. It is perhaps ironic that what this led to would probably make the champions of elitism and exclusivity spin in their (sumptuous) graves. This included the likes of Alcock and Stairs and all those who condemned and humiliated the working lads of Preston – most of who could not afford the expenses incurred by playing the game without some financial compensation.

The promotion of working-class football

It is difficult to imagine a more complete product of inherited money, position and the ideals of Victorian upper-class education than Arnold F. Hills. He shared the belief of his class in the value of sport as character building. This was part the Victorian gospel of hard work and hard play – the 'muscular Christianity' ethos. Sport was part of the moral code of the young men who filled senior positions in the civil service and sat in the boardrooms of industrial enterprises of the Victorian era and this found new expression in the settlement houses and parishes in the poor areas of the cities of Britain. The 'vicars to the poor' took the gospel of sport to their flocks with the same fervour with which their fellow missionaries brought Christianity and 'civilisation' to Africa and Asia, and many of these well-meaning folk used football as a tool in this enterprise.

It was this kind of 'football evangelism', which built on the rational organisation of the game that led, ironically, to the demise of the elitist, amateur enclave of participation in the sport and football eventually became 'the working man's ballet'. The social movement that brought football to the masses would help to break down the class barriers that existed on the field of play. The activity of the likes of Arnold Hills was part of this. Acting the role of wealthy benefactor, Hills was to give Thames Ironworks FC, a team of working men, a major advantage over more experienced football and class rivals.

Whilst the influence of the Old Boy teams on the pitch declined with the coming of professional football, the influence of public school educated administrators on the progress of the game continued to be considerable, and often positive. For example, in the 1880s Lord Kinnaird and C.W. Alcock, both men steeped in the elitist code of association football, had been instrumental in resolving the differences that existed between amateur and professional interests within the game. This compromise, wherein the elite kept the upper hand whilst the 'plebeians' were given a kind of labouring role on the pitch, might be understood as re-entrenchment of class roles given the prevailing environment. It is not too far from what we have in today's professional game. From the player to the fan, from the board member to the kid who wants their club's shirt for Christmas, involvement is dominated by money: the more one has, the higher one's potential level of participation.

—⌐ *Four* ⌐—

The London League
1896/97

Old Castle Swifts had the distinction of being the first professional club in
Essex, and they played on a field hard by the Hermit Road. Their existence
was brief. The Hermit Road 'cinder heap' – it was nothing better – lay
untenanted after their demise, and it was this barren waste that the Thames
Ironworks decided to occupy. A few meetings were called and the project talked
over. Foremen and overseers in the Limited were persuaded to give their
support, a committee was elected, and secretaries appointed. Roughly speaking,
the membership did not exceed fifty.

Syd King (1906) in *The Book of Football*

Around the same time that the Irons were busy entertaining West
Bromwich Albion and Woolwich Arsenal, a meeting was held at
Finsbury Barracks to discuss the formation of a London League. It
was agreed that a competition should be formed made up of both
professional and amateur teams in three divisions. It was hoped that
the new league would help raise the standard of football in London
at a time when clubs from the Midlands and the North-West were
dominating the professional game. Arnold Hills was elected as
president of the new league and Francis Payne, chair of Thames
Ironworks Football Club and an official of the Ironworks Sports

Association, was recruited to a group drafting the first set of rules for the competition.

Thames, although strictly speaking an Essex club, were initially placed in the Second Division of the London League, but they were elevated to the top division after the withdrawal of Royal Ordnance. Secretary Harsent declared in the *Thames Ironworks Gazette* that:

The League will be a new feature in London football next season...it should raise the whole tone of football in the great city.

As the 1896/97 season approached it seemed that Harsent's optimism was well placed. Club membership had increased, enabling the Irons to field three teams. Thames had attracted several new players of renown, including first-teamers from St Luke's and Castle Swifts and four players from Reading, including Davey, Hatton, Rossiter and Holmes. One player who was prevented from joining Thames at this time was an ex-Middlesbrough player called Wynn. Although Wynn was employed at the Ironworks, he was unable to play for the amateur Irons as he had previously been a professional footballer. Inevitably, rumours circulated that Thames were preparing to turn professional, a notion that the club committee was quick to dismiss.

With Harsent standing down as secretary, Francis Payne took over the role as Thames kicked off their first whole season in serious competition. There were thirty first-team matches scheduled and six cup competitions. The Irons' first taste of league action came against Vampires at the Hermit Road ground on 19 September 1896 and resulted in a 3-0 victory for Thames. Seventeen days later the Ironworks side beat the 1st Scots Guards. The reason for the extended period between games was simply that the inaugural London League First Division was comprised of only eight sides.

Despite the promising league form, success in the FA Cup was not forthcoming. In a qualifying round played on 10 October 1896, the Irons were defeated 8-0 at Southern League Sheppy United. Inside-right E.G. Hatton, one of the men brought in from Reading in August, was one of the unhappy Thames side that day. He was to play in all three FA Cup ties for the Irons in the following season. He and his team-mates would have a hard job recovering from this first-hurdle defeat. The sports reporter for the *Courier and Borough of West Ham News* commented:

I do not understand how Sheppy were able to run around Thames by 8-0. Surely the visitors must have been off colour.

Thames were also bundled out of the London Senior Cup 2-0 away to Bromley. Kent was not proving a happy hunting ground for the Irons.

The bad news continued for Thames when they discovered that they were to be evicted from Hermit Road in October 1896. The club had rather blatantly violated its tenancy, according to the ground agent, by in effect building a stadium, including a pavilion. The club had also been guilty of charging admission to games. The home of the Irons was rather eccentric in design. It was surrounded by a moat, to prevent spectators from getting a free view of games. Canvas sheeting had for some time been used as fencing. In those days most matches played by amateur clubs were usually not much more than park affairs. Even the better teams in the district, including Upton Park, marked out the ground with no more than chalk lines around the perimeter of the pitch. Even major FA Cup matches could be watched, for free, by almost anybody. In retrospect, Thames' activity on the site, which was rented purely for playing purposes, seems outrageous, but the men involved with Thames Ironworks Football Club were, by dint of their occupation, constructors. Added to this, in their pursuit of engineering and sport they were also innovators and adventurers, possibly with little interest in the finer points of leasing arrangements. Their activity was also consistent with the growing professionalism of the club. Whilst a culture made up of such individuals had its drawbacks, it may be that the same drives were critical in 'building' the foundations of what was to be the biggest professional sporting organisation in the area and one of the largest of its type in London.

For a time following their eviction, confusion reigned. At one point the club believed that it had been granted a new plot at the same site.

However, the Irons were obliged to play the next four matches on opponents' grounds. Two London Senior Cup ties proved successful, but League points were lost on a visit to the champions-to-be, the 3rd Grenadier Guards. It was five weeks before Arnold Hills secured a temporary home ground for his team at Browning Road, a side street off East Ham High Street. The stay in East Ham didn't get off to the best of starts: the Irons got themselves knocked out of the Essex Senior Cup by Leyton (3-2).

Thames did, however, have a fair run in the London Senior Cup. The kick-off for the third round had to be delayed due to Wandsworth's late arrival. The Irons were leading 7-0 with ten minutes to go when the referee abandoned the game because of bad light. Thames appealed to the London FA asking to be awarded the tie due to their opponent's belated appearance at Browning Road. The South Londoners argued that the fog that stopped the tie was the same fog which had delayed their arrival at the Irons' home ground. The London FA ordered the tie to be replayed. Although Thames were unable to repeat the former rout they won comfortably, seeing off woeful Wandsworth 3-1.

The fifth round occupied the next four Saturdays. The first match against Bromley FC was postponed. The second was abandoned in extra time. The third was undecided after extra time and the fourth went to the London League Second Division club, 2-0.

Overall, the Irons' first team enjoyed little luck in the local cup competitions, and were overshadowed by their reserve side who progressed to a second consecutive West Ham Charity Cup final, losing 1-0 to West Ham Garfield in front of 6,000 spectators at the Spotted Dog Ground in Forest Gate, East London. Bob Heath was the Garfield goalie that day. He must have impressed his opponents. With little delay Thames signed the big, dark, strong 'keeper – who was known to Garfield followers as the Black Panther.

In the London League Thames made good progress, finishing as runners-up to (although well behind) the 3rd Grenadier Guards. The soldiers put a total of nine goals past the Irons in the two League encounters, with Thames managing just one in reply. Much of the credit for the excellent performance of Thames in the London League was attributed to the generosity of Arnold Hills. *The Courier & Borough of West Ham News* declared:

Mr Hills is very liberal with the money and the satisfactory position of the club is almost entirely due to his judicial supervision.

Hills' generosity did not stop with investment in players. In January 1897 he announced that he had found a new home for the Thames Ironworks' football club and athletic societies. He made his announcement at the Thames Ironworks Federated Clubs Annual Festival, remarking that he had secured a large piece of land for an athletic ground and that it would contain a cycle track 'with banking equal to any in London' and that it would also be used for football and tennis. That football was mentioned after cycling – the latter pursuit being a major occupation for the stadium – is revealing. Thames Ironworks Football Club was not considered to be the most important of the Ironworks' societies. The cycling club seems to have been both more popular and more successful. As a result, the grandstand at the new ground would be positioned to give the best view of the home straight.

The new ground was to be situated in Plaistow. In order that it could be opened in June 1897 to commemorate the sixtieth year of Queen Victoria's reign, the stadium site was turned from a wilderness into an arena equal to any in the country in just fourteen weeks. This was a magnificent achievement that would be hard to match in modern terms. The Memorial Ground, named in honour of Her Royal Majesty's anniversary, could accommodate more than 100,000 spectators and was constructed at a cost of more than £20,000 – an astronomical sum just before the turn of the twentieth century. It provided a clubhouse and sports complex that included plans to build an outdoor swimming pool that would be over 100 feet in length and given over for the use of the Thames Ironworks employees. The cycle track, which was a third of a mile in circumference, skirted a cinder running track that itself encompassed the football pitch. The opening of the new ground attracted 8,000 people, who came to see a varied programme of events that included polo and cock fighting.

The Memorial Ground was situated close to the future site of West Ham station – but this didn't open until 1901. The location still retains a sporting connection in the twenty-first century, being the home of East London Rugby Club.

The Irons made their debut at the Memorial Ground shortly after the grand opening on Jubilee Day, in a friendly against Northfleet, but only 200 spectators turned up. As the rain began to fall on the ragged little band of supporters strung out around the huge ground, the secretary, Payne, sent out the invitation to every spectator to move undercover in the grandstand. It was a poor showing for a ground that Payne described as being good enough to hold the Cup Final. Indeed, it was to be considered for the 1901 FA Cup semi-final, Tottenham Hotspur *v*. West Bromwich Albion.

Disappointing support was something the Irons were growing used to. This was surprising in that after only two years Thames had become one of the top teams in an area that was described in *Association Football and the Men Who Made it* (1905) as 'football mad' with 'hundreds of urchins kicking balls in the streets'. Disappointment that so few men from the Ironworks attended matches was expressed in the *Thames Ironworks Gazette*:

The support we have received has not been so large as we should wish for, the gates not totalling near the number we might expect and certainly not so many as the quality of the play of our men should warrant.

It was hard for the club organisers to understand why so many people went to matches at grounds that were,

...much less pleasing and where the football is nowhere near as good...Things will have to improve when people realise how splendid the ground is and how good the club is...

These remarks reveal what the club had become and possibly account, however unconsciously, for its lack of support. Thames could hardly expect to be well supported by Ironworks employees when its path to professionalism was taking it ever further from being a works team. Workers could gain membership to the club – this allowed them to attend training on Tuesday and Thursday evenings and take part in practice matches – but there was no suggestion that they would be considered for a place in the team. As such, Ironworks employees could have no hope of taking an active playing part in the main function of the club: the winning of games against first-class opposition. Thames had incorporated leading local clubs and was winning, but it had no particular constituency to whom it could appeal. It was not representative on any particular area of West Ham, and it only had a nominal tie with the Ironworks. The Irons had no trouble defeating their local rivals on the field. They had a long record of remaining undefeated by any amateur team, but this did not ensure success at the gate.

To gain support the committee had, almost from the start, decided to attempt to produce high quality football and this meant becoming more professional. Large crowds would only be attracted if professional clubs came to play competitively at the Memorial Ground, but the club was never going to come anywhere near filling its massive home stadium whilst it was converting Thames into a competent professional side that could compete at the highest level. The Irons needed to buy time. This was made possible by the continuing patronage of Arnold Hills. Hills was to supplement the club's income well into its maturation as a professional entity, but it would have been unlikely, at this early juncture, that he would have been willing to subsidise an openly fully professional side. As such, it was perhaps not surprising that the committee held back on admitting professional ambitions.

Surprisingly, Hills remained tolerant of the obviously growing professionalism of Thames Ironworks Football Club, the sporting progeny of his puritan paternalism. Why did he continue to nurture the football club long after it had ceased to play the role he had envisioned for it? It could no longer be regarded as a cementing factor within a harmonious industrial community and had lost its role in creating solidarity and identity with the firm.

— Five —

Hot Iron and Ships

Friends of the winter game,
Patrons assembled here,
Most proud are we to name
The favourites we hold dear;
Then let a 'three times three'
From this vast concourse rise,
And laud both loud and heartily,
The stalwart West Ham boys,
Whose claim to fame can not be slighted
So long as they remain 'United'.

From *May West Ham still remain United* by AC – Cricket Rhymester

In 1837, Queen Victoria succeeded her uncle, William IV, and became Queen of England. She was only eighteen years of age. Just three years before the shipwright Thomas Ditchburn, who had been involved in shipbuilding at Rotherhithe, and naval architect Charles J. Mare joined forces to found the first iron shipbuilding yard on the River Thames. They called it, unsurprisingly, Ditchburn and Mare. The modest location was laid out on the south side of the river at Deptford. After a fire gutted the yard, they transferred to the northern bank of the Thames, taking over a five-acre defunct shipbuilding premises along

Orchard Place between the East India Dock Basin and the mouth of the river Lea, more often referred to at this point as Bow Creek, where the Thames curves away from the Isle of Dogs at Blackwall.

Shipbuilding had taken place at Blackwall since 1587, but the confined nature of the spit meant that only ships of less than 1,000 tons could be built there. In the first part of the nineteenth century there was a lack of convenient rail links to the immediate area and this made the cost of bringing in iron plate from the north prohibitive, and also meant that the delivery of raw materials was often delayed. Mare saw that smelting wrought-iron plate and building rolling mills on site could alleviate these difficulties. However, if this ambition were to be made a reality the company would have to move to a larger location that would allow for what would be an appreciable expansion of the plant.

Charles Mare identified a site with the potential to facilitate what he saw as the necessary growth of the company, an area of open land, just across Bow Creek on the eastern bank of the River Lea where it meets the River Thames in the Borough of West Ham, Essex. However, Mare's partner, Thomas Ditchburn, didn't feel secure about this location, as it would be subjected to flooding from spring high tides. The River Lea at Silvertown Way in those days was 50ft wide at low water but over 200ft wide at high tide. For all this, Mare was so keen to undertake this new venture that he changed the nature of his partnership with Ditchburn and purchased around ten acres of marshland for a new, larger yard on the northern, Canning Town bank of the Lea.

Mare staked out the site personally, aided by a young apprentice, Clement Mackrow, who was to become naval architect to Thames Ironworks. By 1843 two new slips capable of taking four ships each were staked out for the purpose of building small iron steamers for the Citizen Ship Company. However, the original site of the Thames Ironworks, which was also to continue to be known as Ditchburn and Mare for much of the rest of the century, was to produce several innovative iron racing yachts – the most famous, the *Mosquito*, was built in 1846. She was an impressive 70-footer with a 15ft 2in beam.

She is included in the *Guinness Book of Yachting Facts*. This was the start of West Ham United Football Club's nautical heritage.

The second half of the nineteenth century saw a revolution in communications. In 1840 Samuel Morse patented his invention of the code that bears his name. The telegraph spread rapidly in the next ten years. It was also a time of Colonial expansion and struggle. The Battle of Blood River took place in 1838, and concluded in the defeat of the Zulus by the Boers in Natal, South Africa. The British occupied Aden in 1839 and the Opium war between Britain and China, which was to last until 1842, began. Britain was also involved in protracted and bloody hostilities in Afghanistan. Turkey invaded Syria and was heavily defeated in the Battle of Nesib. There were rebellions in Upper and Lower Canada whilst New Zealand was in the process of becoming a British Crown Colony. This was ratified in 1840 under the Treaty of Waitagi. At around the same time the Treaty of London was signed, whereby Britain, Russia, Prussia and Austria agreed to limit Egyptian expansion. The British Navy bombarded Beirut and the penny post was introduced in Britain.

All this made it a good time for the shipbuilding industry and throughout the 1850s and into the 1860s East London firms in Limehouse, Millwall and Blackwall – being the first to have adjusted to the demand for large iron vessels – flourished. It was during this period, in 1853, that the P&O transport ship *The Himalaya* was launched. It was very much a milestone in the history of Thames Ironworks. At 5,500 tonnes she was, at that time, the biggest merchant ship in the world. Her construction was an outstanding achievement for the yard, showing the potential that Thames Ironworks had to build ships on the most grandiose scale. *The Himalaya* became a troopship in the Crimean War (1854-56) and was still in Admiralty service off Portland when she was sunk by German bombing in the Second World War.

As the second half of the century moved on, Mare's firm prospered and expanded. At its height it was a thirty-acre primal industrial park, split into two sites surrounding either side of Bow Creek. It was more than capable of undertaking the largest contracts up to a capacity of 25,000 tonnes of warships and 10,000 tonnes of first-class mail steamers at the same time. Orchard Place, which remained the company's registered address until 1903, was linked to the main shipbuilding base in Canning Town by a chain ferry. At the zenith of its development this mechanism was capable of transporting 200 men at a time across Bow Creek – this was quite an engineering feat in itself, and showed that the company was a major employer in the area.

Mare was fast building a reputation for inventive maritime design and development. He built the first screw-driven ship for the Royal Navy, Queen Victoria's Royal Yacht *Fairy*. The propeller drive of the *Fairy* was far less noisy than the paddle steamer it replaced and avoided the vibration formally experienced in the Royal apartments. The Queen showed her relief and gratitude by offering Mare a knighthood, but he was reported to have 'modestly declined'. This was an odd reaction, particularly at the time when the distinction of a knighthood would have opened many doors to Charles Mare. Of course there are a number or reasons why he might have spurned aristocratic recognition, his politics or religion for instance, but it might be more likely that the young monarch may have acted a little too spontaneously for the taste of her political advisors. Little is known of Charles Mare's background, but he does appear to have come from an artisan class, perhaps with Irish connections. As such his 'modesty' may have at least been a convenient response for those who wished to preserve Royal favours for a certain class or 'type' of person.

For all this, and maybe partly because of it, Thames Ironworks continued to capture lucrative and prestigious contracts, although the company was not without its competitors on the Thames. Millwall Ironworks were involved in a number of the same markets as their neighbours in Canning Town. Millwall smelted their steel from iron ore and rolled it. Thames Ironworks reconstituted scrap and, appropriately, hammered it. The competition was fierce, at times manifesting itself in running battles between employees from the rival works. Ironworkers were tough and often rugged types, a volatile mixture of working-class Scots, Irish and Cockneys. When they made war on the streets it would be no mere scuffle. This was not the equivalent of a teenage, last orders fracas. Combat between ironworkers was a conflict between men, hard as iron. It was rare and real. Hostility could be tasted on the river air well before a battle commenced. As such there was a passionate rivalry between West Ham and Millwall that pre-empted the beautiful game. The ancestors of the Lions, Millwall Rovers, were not in fact Ironworkers, but a group of mostly Scotsmen employed at the jam and marmalade makers J.T. Morton's at West Ferry Road on the Isle of Dogs. As such it is perhaps not surprising that West Ham have had Millwall on toast so many times ...

By 1856 Mare was in charge of one of Britain's leading civil engineering concerns, but he ran into some considerable financial difficulties due to miscalculations on a contract for a number of gunboats. Money troubles were exacerbated by problems involving some work on bridges. After a brief financial struggle, the firm was on the point of bankruptcy. Peter Rolt, a timber merchant and Mare's father-in-law, stepped in and suggested that the company should be turned over to him. The firm would still retain the name Thames Ironworks but Rolt wanted to add 'shipbuilding and engineering' to the company title. Mare readily agreed and Rolt, who was also Mare's major creditor, purchased the assets and assigned them to a new limited liability company, established under the Limited Liability Act that had then recently been passed by Parliament. This action prevented one of the largest employers on the Thames from being broken up.

In 1858 the French Navy launched the *Gloire*, a wood- and-iron hulled ship. At this time all British naval vessels were totally wooden hulled. Although there were many iron-hulled merchant ships at this time, the Navy had been cautious about the use of iron. In testing, when hit by shellfire, ships girdled in metal would splinter – threatening to inflict fearful and complicated injuries on the crew. However, the French advance obliged Britain to respond and an order was then placed with Thames Ironworks to build the world's first all iron-hulled warship, that would also be the biggest fighting vessel ever to sail the seas. Rolt's company won the order against stiff competition because of the quality of its own wrought-iron plate and the firm's experience of building ships in this material.

The 9,000 tonne-plus ship was given the name *Warrior*, epitomising her practical and psychological purpose. She was launched on 29 December 1860. It was a bitterly cold day. The shipyard workers had been up all night keeping the ways clear of snow and ice. Lord Palmerston, the Navy surveyor, performed the launching ceremony at 2.30 p.m. *HMS Warrior* was then pulled by tugs into Victoria Dock where she spent a year being fitted out and having her engines installed. Penn and Sons of Greenwich, then the leaders in the development and design of nautical engines, supplied the propulsion units.

With the success of the *Warrior*, orders came in from navies around the world. The impact this ship made cannot be underestimated. She made the Thames Ironworks one of the world's most famous shipbuilding and engineering companies.

The river surrounding the Thames Ironworks was a lively area in the company's developmental years. Many of the local people earned their living from and on the water. Their combined skills, generated from working in a collection of industries, were used to convert former lifeboats, whalers and other antiquated craft into suitable vessels for use on the river, ferrying goods and passengers to and from wharves up and down the banks. At the mouth of the Thames, the waves were harvested for whitebait, shrimps and cockles and transported up to Billingsgate fish market for sale. 'Toshing' (collecting rubbish) was also a profitable pursuit. The swift running tide near the entrance of Bow Creek, close to Orchard Place, would sweep into Bugsby's Reach and carry ashore baulks of timber and other salvageable materials together with items that had fallen from the huge amount of traffic that plied the Thames in those times, from life-boats to gold watches (or 'yellow kettles' as they were called: kettle was another word for gun metal, and watches were commonly made out of this material). According to the law, anything salvaged had to be delivered to Dead Man's Wharf at Deptford to await reclamation, but the prize for honesty was so negligible and slow to materialise that most of the fruits of the toshers' labours were recycled locally.

As Thames Ironworks took on more and more projects, building ships in wood and iron and later steel, the company began to expand both in terms of the expertise it commanded and its product. The reputation embodied in the *Warrior* generated demand and the yard built the first iron-hulled warships for Spain, Russia, Portugal, Greece, Turkey and Denmark. In 1870 the company completed an order for the first iron-hulled ship to serve in the Prussian Navy, the *König Wilhelm*, which was very similar to the *Warrior* in dimension and design. She became Germany's longest serving warship, fighting the cause of her country through the First World War and beyond, up to 1926.

As the new century approached, management and workers from all the major maritime nations came to Canning Town to share in the latest advances in shipbuilding. The works was visited by many of the Crown Heads of Europe, including the Kaiser who came to England in the Ironworks' own *König Wilhelm* for the Silver Jubilee of his grandmother, Queen Victoria. During his stay, the *König Wilhelm*, that had by now seen its first year of service, was placed in the hands of Thames Ironworks for a dry-dock hull inspection.

Thames Ironworks continued to do business, whilst the yards around them were collapsing. Shipbuilding in the East London area had been in decline since the end of 1866. Early in 1867, *The Times* reported that 30,000 unemployed people were seeking relief in Poplar, many of these coming from the shipbuilding industry that just a few months earlier had employed 15,000 men and boys. Thames Ironworks probably had their diversity and reputation to thank for their continued prosperity. Many of the company's employees must have counted their blessings in the hard winter of 1867. For the third time in twelve years there were bread riots in the most hard-hit districts, and there were even problems in areas hitherto thought of as lower middle class in nature.

This was the industrial foundation on which Thames Ironworks Football Club was to be built and developed. It is also the background of the first years of West Ham United.

~ Six ~

The Boys from the Memorial Grounds 1897/98

They had to move from Hermit Road, though, the next year and they subsequently appeared at Browning Road, East Ham. For some reason, not altogether explained, the local public at this place did not take kindly to them, and the records show that Browning Road was a wilderness both in the matter of luck and support. Still there was a bright time coming, it was thought, and people were beginning to talk about the Memorial Ground at Canning Town. This vast athletic enclosure was built by Mr Hills, and, if my memory is not at fault, I think it was opened on Jubilee Day, 1897. History had been made at the Memorial Ground. Troubles and triumphs are associated with the enclosure, but, somehow, West Ham never succeeded there as it was once thought they would. Thames Ironworks, however, won the London League championship in 1898.

Syd King (1906) in *The Book of Football*

Just before the new season the Thames Ironworks Football Club committee took the bold step of insuring players against loss of earnings resulting from injuries, thus taking yet another step towards full professionalism. However, club officials were still saying that they were on this road, probably looking to keep the financial support of Arnold Hills flowing until the club was able to be self sufficient.

Six new players were signed for the 1887/98 season – five of these were from the Greater London area, but none of them worked for the Ironworks. The single local player to break into the side was 'keeper George Furnell. Once associated with Old Castle Swifts, Furnell was to only stay at the Memorial Ground for the 1897/98 term, but he played in all three of Thames' FA Cup ties in that season and was a regular in the London League side. He was transferred to Hammersmith Athletic. Other new names included Henry Hird from Stockton, who recorded twenty-two outings for Thames between April 1898 and October 1899, netting three times in the 1898/99 season. George Neill came in from West Norwood at the age of twenty-two and could play at wing-half or wing-back. He is credited with appearing twenty-six times for Thames, putting the ball between the posts on four occasions. Like most other players at this time, George would have probably played more times than indicated in the records, but match statistics were not all that well attended to at the time of his arrival at Thames in 1897. It is known that he first appeared in a Thames XI in the London League and played regularly until the end of 1898.

The Irons sported their new kit when they kicked off their first competitive season at the Memorial Ground. The strip consisted of Royal Cambridge blue shirts, white knickers, red cap, belt and stockings. The *Thames Ironworks Gazette* commented that when the new colours were worn on the field 'The contrast supplied by the delightful green turf is very pleasing'. From time to time Thames would also play in a Harrovian blue strip (a mid-to-dark blue, which appears to have been the side's original strip, consistent with Hills' school and university colours).

Thames also gained some pleasing results. In September the Irons limited Millwall Rovers, a strong professional Southern League side, to a 2-0 margin. Tommy Moore played in goal for the Lions in that game, although his esoteric skills were to serve Thames in the following two seasons. Moore was to guard the Thames goal line some sixty-one times. He came in to cover for Hughie Monteith on four occasions during West Ham United's first season in the Southern League. Known as the 'Dancing Dervish' because of his unconventional methods of evading challenging forwards, Moore was not without his critics, but he managed to attain a fair level of consistency during his time at the Memorial Ground and missed only two Southern League matches in that period. Tommy was to be exiled to the backwater of Grays early in 1901. He seemed destined to disappear from the limelight, but in the FA Cup of the following season he gave an inspired display of goalkeeping and was largely responsible for the Essex village team's shock 2-1 second qualifying round win, on a foggy November afternoon at the Memorial Ground.

In the second game of the new season, Leyton were given a 4-0 beating at the Memorial, following which football correspondent TAM wrote in the *Morning Leader:*

Nearly 2,000 spectators saw the match, which was commenced by the Ironworks in real earnest. Twenty-five minutes after the start the Ironworks, who so far had the best of matters, obtained their first point in the following manner: Hatton secured about fifty yards from goal and after dodging and wriggling through the whole of the Leyton defence, tested Sterling with a stinger that was only partially cleared and Hatton, pouncing on the ball again, promptly rushed it through.

Three minutes later, Gresham scored a second, so enabling the Thames to cross over with a deserved lead of two goals. For the best part of the game it was Thames forwards v. Leyton's defence and although beaten twice before the finish by Reid and Edwards, they were in no way disgraced.

Hatton was the most conspicuous of the Ironworks forwards, while Dove, Neill, Dandridge and Chisholm all played well in defence with goalkeeper Furnell having a very easy task. (Wednesday 6 October 1897)

By November the East Londoners topped the London League, having won their first six games.

The first FA Cup tie played at the Memorial Ground was a preliminary round match that brought a 3-0 victory over Redhill. Simon (Peter) Chisholm from Inverness got two of his total of three goals for the club that day. Chisholm, known as the 'Laughing Jock' because of his convivial attitude at the end of games, win or lose, was to be with Thames until the spring of 1899, recording twenty-two appearances.

After beating Royal Engineers Thames Battalion in the second qualifying round, the Irons were eliminated 2-0 at Southern League St Albans. It was the third season in succession that Thames had been knocked out by a Southern League club.

A 3-1 defeat at the Memorial in a local derby against Ilford in the third round of the London Senior Cup was the last real low point of the season. Thames had scored seven in two games against the west Essex side and had been expected to go through. It was a real shock result, causing fear in some quarters that this might be the start of a Thames decline.

James Reid, an inside-forward from Reading and formally with Port Vale and Hibernian, was in the Irons XI that started the game. One of the many pre-season signings, Jimmy was to record nineteen appearances for Thames between 1897 and 1900, notching up twelve goals according to the rather sporadically kept record books of the time. He played in West Ham United's first season, taking to the field nineteen times for the Hammers and getting on the score-sheet five times in that initial Southern League First Division season.

Thames switched their focus to the London League. The Irons faced high-flying Brentford at Shotters Field in their penultimate game of this competition. It was a crucial encounter between the two main contenders for the championship. Just before the match, the *East Ham Echo* published a feature entitled 'Football Sketches – 1 Charlie Dove (Thames Ironworks)'. The anonymous author wrote:

If not absolutely the finest right half-back in Essex, the subject of our sketch is undoubtedly one of the most brilliant men in the country in that position. Born just over nineteen years ago, Charles Dove first began his football career with Park School – a team that has always been classed as on of the finest schoolboy combinations. There he figured at full-back and just by way of encouragement won two medals when playing in this position.

Leaving school life he migrated to Forest Swift Juniors as a centre forward and subsequently captained Plaistow Melville.

He also figured in the lines of Upton Park and South West Ham and three seasons ago joined the ranks of Thames Ironworks and has played with them ever since.

Even when joining his true position was not apparent. He played centre forward and full-back and it was not until he had occupied nearly every place – with the exception of goal – that his worth as a right half was demonstrated.

In this berth he plays a brilliant game, full of resource, and the Thames Limited combination sadly missed him in their opening matches. However, he is expected to be fit and able to turn out on Saturday against Brentford, when he will considerably strengthen the team.

Charles Dove was one of only two Thames players from the team's early days at Hermit Road who had retained their places in the first team. He had joined Thames at the age of sixteen in 1895, having served as an apprentice at the shipyard. Standing nearly six feet in height and tipping the scales at twelve stone, Charlie was popular with the supporters, representing home-grown, local talent. In a winning game against Maidenhead on the final day of 1898 he played in goal and kept Irons in the Southern League Second Division championship. Dove was transferred to the Irons' great rivals of the Edwardian era, Millwall, in September 1901, but a knee injury in the 1902/03 season ended his first-class career. He was to record forty-one matches for the Irons and got three goals in the 1898/99 term. Dove had sixteen games in claret and blue.

The other long-term Iron was George Gresham, an inside-forward. Just twenty-three years of age at the end of the 1897/98 season, George was the first of many players to join Thames from the Lincolnshire club Gainsborough Trinity, turning out fifteen times for the Irons in their first season. He scored twice against Woolwich Arsenal in the 'Floodlight Friendly' of 3 March 1896 and was another player to figure in the three FA Cup ties of 1897/98. In the 1898/99 Southern League Second Division campaign, George battled through eighteen matches in Thames colours, bagging five goals in the process.

Thames were beaten 1-0 by Brentford. It was their first defeat of the season. So, everything depended on the final games of the League competition. Thames faced the 2nd Grenadier Guards, whilst Brentford lined up against Barking Woodville. If the Bees won their match against the Essex boys the championship would go to West London no matter what the Irons did, but Thames had to make sure they defeated the Pongos. The Irons won well, sending the soldiers back to their billets and barracks on the end of a 3-1 thrashing. News didn't travel too fast at the latter end of the nineteenth century, but it wasn't too long after the game that Thames found out that Barking and Woodville had done their Essex neighbours a good turn and beaten Brentford. The Irons were, by a single point, champions, pushing Brentford into the runners-up spot. Thames had only surrendered 5 points out of a possible 32 in sixteen games, averaging just under three goals per match. They had lost just once.

The Irons had achieved some excellent performances during their highly successful London League campaign. Bromley had been beaten 7-3 and 5-1 – ample revenge for the previous season's London Cup defeat – and the boys from the Memorial Ground had also 'done the double' over the 3rd Grenadier Guards, thus reversing the previous season's fortunes.

The club captain of the title-winning side was Teesider Walter Tranter. He had a reputation for rushing in where others feared to tread. Walley played at left-back in the Thames team that season. Amid the celebrations at the presentation concert to honour the triumph, Walley 'by mistake' carried off the Dewar Shield, another major trophy, but not rightfully the property of the Irons or Walley. He did, eventually, return the silverware. The Middlesbrough-born defender was to lead Thames twenty-five times in their championship-winning Southern League Second Division campaign the following season, but surprisingly joined Chatham at the start of the 1899/1900 term. He returned to the Memorial Ground for the 1900/01 campaign, wearing the Hammers over his heart on six occasions. Tranter later went on to play in Northern Ireland for a Belfast club. Walley was to gain representative honours, playing for the London League against the London Football Association alongside team-mate George Neil in

December 1897 at Kilburn. Jimmy Reid was also selected as a reserve. These appear to be the first Thames players to receive any kind of representative recognition.

In April 1898 Thames rounded off a glorious season with a friendly against Woolwich Arsenal, a side which at that time was highly placed in the Football League Second Division. There has never really been such a thing as a 'friendly' between these London clubs and this was confirmed when Arsenal took the field with nine of their regular League side plus two new signings. Following a hard-fought eighty minutes of play, Thames found themselves leading their illustrious opponents 2-1. In desperation the Gunners almost recklessly threw everything at the Irons defence and, as would so often be the case in the future with 'lucky Arsenal', they saved their blushes with a last-ditch effort.

—⌒ Seven ⌒—

The *Albion*

The time was ripe for a limited liability company, and the public were shortly afterwards invited to take up shares. Next year the name was changed from Thames Ironworks to West Ham United, and henceforward the doors of the club were open to the rank and file.

Syd King (1906) in *The Book of Football*

At the end of the 1897/98 season, the splendid facilities at the Memorial Ground and the enlistment of better players energised the ambitions of the committee of Thames Ironworks FC. This, together with success of their team, boosted their confidence to the extent that they determined to more openly embrace professionalism in an attempt to increase the sparse population of the their home ground.

The committee decided to approach Hills with a range of proposals that would effectively change the amateur profile of the club. Hills, as an advocate of 'sport for sport's sake', must have found the suggestion that players should be blatantly paid a wage, rather than just receive expenses or compensation, quite unpalatable. Following protracted debate he agreed to the committee's propositions, but with the greatest reluctance. It is difficult to understand why he compromised his deeply-held convictions, but at this juncture Hills was recovering from the tragedy that surrounded the launch of the ship which embodied the hope and future of Thames Ironworks.

The *Albion* was a first-class cruiser that had been ordered by the Navy. The Admiralty had commissioned her from Thames Ironworks at the height of the 'naval race' in Europe as the Continent started the slow build-up to war. She had been completed slightly behind schedule: the yard was suffering from a staff shortage and an engineering union strike, centred on the cause of the 'eight-hour day', was affecting supplying contractors and disrupting delivery dates. The workers at Thames Ironworks had not taken part in the engineers' actions, Hills having introduced the eight-hour day some years earlier.

The *Albion*, one of the Royal Navy's last pre-dreadnought battleships, was 800 tonnes lighter than her original design had stipulated, due to the failure of government-employed contractors to supply the correct level of armour plating to clad the ship, but being 390ft long and 74ft wide, she still weighed in a massive 6,000 tonnes. Launches were not unusual events at the yard, but then the *Albion* was no ordinary ship. She was British, and that was seen as something to celebrate on 21 June 1898, as was the fact that she would be the first Thames Ironworks ship to be launched by Royal hand. Although a local newspaper reported that no fewer than 100,000 people attended the launch, probably nearer 30,000 people crammed around the yard to watch the Duke and Duchess of York (soon to be King George V and Queen Mary) give the massive vessel her title. The shipyard was covered in bunting and flags and excitement was mounting as the 3 p.m. launch time approached. Yard workers and local school children were given the day off to attend the event and families dressed in their best clothes. Employees received a special bonus on the day, one shilling for apprentices, half a crown and a straw hat for shipwrights. The afternoon was bathed in golden sunshine and this increased the carnival atmosphere. Around 20,000 tickets had been given to Ironworks employees, but the men on the yard gate were told to let in anyone who looked 'respectable'. Management had arranged for seventy policemen to help with crowd control, far too few to have anything but the most minimal impact on the mass of people jostling around and seeking the best view of the occasion.

A narrow workmen's slipway running by the side of the nearly-finished Japanese warship the *Shikisima* provided the best view of events. Workers at the yard knew the bridge had not been designed to take the weight of any sizeable number of people and had put a sign up indicating the danger of using it, but as the afternoon drew on and the crowd grew more anxious to find a good vantage point, the police, who up to this point had kept the bridge clear, allowed over 200 people to squeeze onto it. The *East Ham Echo* described the situation:

As the time for the ceremony approached the crowd grew denser, and just after the Royal party and the other guests of the company had left the luncheon table, a rush took place for the bridge at the bottom of the middle slip. The temptation was a great one. There was no one there, and the place was clear of scaffolding except on the left, where the towering sides of the Japanese battleship rose many feet in the air. The warnings of experienced workmen and officials of the company were unheeded and, bearing down all opposition, the people swarmed on to the frail bridge. Most of them were women and children.

When the Royal entourage arrived at the yard, which was festooned in a kaleidoscope of colours, they had lunch with Arnold J. Hills, Lady Mary Lyon, Sir Charles Cust, the Venerable Archdeacon Stevens, Canon Pelly and other dignitaries. The atmosphere was enjoyably tense and expectant.

As much as anything else the occasion was a right of passage for Hills. He had never been offered the type of honour turned down by Charles Mare, the yard's founder, and the completion of the *Albion* was his chance to break into the ranks of the aristocracy, the one privilege to evade his family. This was his moment, the zenith of a lifetime of work in industry and philanthropic activity. He had been a good servant to industry, working intelligently with his employees and making every effort to recruit them to the cause of company, capital, Britain and the Empire.

Following hurried consultation with the company's engineers it was decided to bring the launch time forward to 2.50 p.m. as the dogshores supporting the ship looked like they were giving way and a collapse seemed imminent. The Royal guests and other dignitaries gathered under a canopy headstage close to the bows of the great ship. The Duchess sent the champagne bottle hurtling toward the hull but it failed to shatter. Two more times she tried, but still not a drop of alcohol touched the *Albion*. In exasperation she gave up and cut the cord. The ship had, as such, not been 'blessed' – which would have been considered amongst shipbuilders an almost blasphemous flouting of tradition and practically a curse on any vessel.

The cutting of the cord was the signal to the workmen to release the dogshores. George Clement Macrow, the shipbuilding manager, had expected the *Albion* to move into the creek at speed and it did, creating a massive surge of water. As she hit the water, the *Albion* displaced a tidal wave that smashed the slipway into a thousand pieces. With no time to escape, spectators on the crowded gantry alongside the *Shikisima* were thrown into the muddy, churning waters around the *Albion,* the cheering of the thousands that saw the *Albion* descend into Bow Creek drowning their cries for help. At that point few people had any idea tht a tragedy had occurred. The Duke and Duchess certainly did not. From the Royal Grandstand at the bow of the vessel, nothing could be seen of the starboard side of the *Albion*, the site of the calamity.

As soon as their task was completed, the Royal party quickly returned to the launch they had arrived in, completely oblivious to the desperate struggle that was taking place in water just ten feet deep and five yards from shore. Many of the thirty-eight people who died were trapped underneath timbers or concussed by floating baulks or other debris that had fallen into the water from the slipway. Others were trampled by groups of people desperately trying to reach safety. Nearby spectators and shipyard workers did their best to rescue people in the water, diving into the creek to drag out survivors, but it was more than ten minutes before the shipyard managers knew anything about the disaster. As soon as they did, Thames policemen in rowing boats were dispatched to bring victims ashore, where the Metropolitan Police and the Fire Brigade were doing their best for the injured and dying, and to prevent further chaos.

At first nobody realised that people had died, but the reality soon became horrifyingly clear. Sub-Divisional Inspector Dixon of the Thames Police was to tell the inquest:

... for a time officials thought everyone had been safely recovered ... then one, and another, and another body came to the water's surface.

An hour or so after the accident, workmen began to drag the river and the shipyard diver, Bill Hodgson, was lowered into the dark water to check for bodies trapped in the mud. The body count was twenty-four by 5.30 p.m. A mortuary had been set up in an engineering department shed. The St Katherine's Homes nurses and Dr Humphries checked for signs of life. The nurses covered each body with a sheet, washed the bodies and replaced wet and damage clothes with clean outfits that had been swiftly brought to the yard. The suits and dresses that the victims died in, their 'Sunday best', were left in a bundle at the feet of each corpse to aid identification by relatives. PC Lambert took descriptions of the victims before they were covered with canvas.

A more suitable mortuary was soon required. The shipyard workers erected wooden benches in an old galvanising shed while electrician Fred Wilson installed lighting. By 7.00 p.m. the bodies were moved from the engineering shed. When Fred Wilson turned on the lights he had installed in the makeshift mortuary, his eyes fell upon the lifeless form of his sister Matilda, who had recently married and just returned from her honeymoon. Not far from her, Fred found his dead mother.

When news of the tragedy spread, a crowd gathered outside the Ironworks but only relatives and friends of the deceased were allowed in. The search for victims went on as darkness fell over the river. By midnight distressed relatives had identified twenty–nine victims. Three others awaited recognition.

The day after the accident, West Ham Council opened a fund to help survivors and the bereaved. Canning Town, the area most directly affected by the disaster, was a desperately poor district. Even some of those who had got away with little more than a drenching had seen what few good clothes they possessed ruined.

Hills was overcome with grief and, in the days and weeks following the disaster, he visited bereaved families and promised to meet funeral expenses that would have otherwise financially crippled many. He was to write:

I went out to the homes of those who had lost dear ones and shared with them of the grief that filled our hearts. I found the sweetest solace for all. For I met with no shadow of bitterness – no tone of complaint.

He went on to express his feelings of personal responsibility:

I represented the company at whose doors the responsibility of this great accident lay; but none the less the mother weeping for her child, the husband heartbroken for the loss of his young wife, clasped my hand, and in broken accents told me how sorry they were that this terrible accident should have marred all the joyous festivities. I can make no fit recompense, but I pray to God that so long as He may spare me I may be enabled to do something for the well-being and happiness of Canning Town.

Within twenty-four hours Hills had purchased a large plot in East London Cemetery. He planned a grandiose memorial involving a rolling wave and an angel, but the Disaster Fund Committee felt that the money that had been collected for the families of the victims should not be spent on stonework. Two engraved tablets set apart from the surroundings by an anchor mark the grave. It can still be found in the cemetery today, the final resting place of twenty-eight victims. Others were buried in individual graves in different parts of the cemetery or interred at other graveyards.

The *Albion* had been launched on a Tuesday; the dead were buried on the following Saturday, Monday and Tuesday. Scenes at the funerals were harrowing. Huge crowds lined the routes that the different funeral cortèges took. Mrs Eliza Tarbot, at sixty-four years of age, was the oldest person to lose her life in the catastrophe. She was the first to be buried. Mrs Isabel White, who was thirty, was next to be interred. She was found in the water with her two small daughters still clutching at her skirts; both the little girls also lost their lives.

The police were criticised for having insufficient officers on duty at the launch, although the inquest later heard that the management of the Ironworks had calculated the number of police needed. However, 15,000 officers attended the Saturday funeral. On the Monday

7,000 turned up, whilst the Tuesday service saw around 5,000 on duty. Clearly the authorities were more careful about the need to control and deter possible protest than they were in taking responsibility for the policing of community events.

It was only very recently, with the building of Canning Town Station, part of the Docklands Light Railway, that a plaque was put in place to record the fact that the Ironworks stood on the riverbank at Canning Town. There is no memorial to those who lost their lives at the launch of the *Albion*.

The show must go on

Arnold Hills was never to be the same man as he was before the disaster. Perhaps this explains why he didn't put up more of a fight against Thames Ironworks Football Club becoming professional; maybe the disaster had caused him to develop his perspective on life and see that sport was relatively insignificant in the scheme of things.

Whatever the case, the Thames committee were determined not to rest on their laurels. With the London League title not yet dry from the celebratory champagne, the committee secured a place in the Second Division of the Southern League, where the likes of Fulham and Watford, as well as their recent sparring partner Brentford, awaited them. The Irons also entered the Thames & Medway Combination for the 1898/99 season. Elevation to the Southern League meant that the club required a more professional approach, but the team was still struggling to attract big crowds. The Memorial Ground had always been difficult to get to and Thames had continued to fail to appeal to any particular community that was capable of supplying the necessary core support for a professional club. All too often the committee had been forced to go cap in hand to Arnold Hills. A letter to the *Thames Ironworks Gazette* from the club secretary summed up the situation:

I regret to say that from a financial point of view it has been a hard struggle. We are much indebted to the kindness of our president, who from time to time has assisted us in paying our debts, but it is very discouraging to us to feel that we have little or no support from the Works and that among the many admirers of football in Canning Town, so few attend our matches.

A lack of support, however, would not get in the way of the committee's ambition to reach the First Division of the Southern League at the first attempt. Although Walter Tranter remained as skipper, he was one of only three players (out of thirty) who were retained from the victorious London League campaign. Twenty-seven new players were engaged, many of them professionals. Although the administrative and financial connections with the Ironworks were maintained, this overt leap towards total professionalism as good as severed any remaining community links with the Ironworks.

The new players were attracted from far and wide – among them were four Scots and a Welshman – so the side were also losing their East End associations. There are no records of the players' wages, but it would be naïve to think that they were attracted from professional clubs as far away as Middlesbrough, Aberystwyth and Inverness just to take in the sights, sounds and smells of Canning Town. Amongst the new recruits was David Lloyd who, at 6ft 4in and 13st, came along with three others from the 3rd Grenadier Guards. Lloyd was to bag twelve goals in fourteen games during his one season playing in the cup and Southern League, making him Thames' top marksman in 1898/99.

As they marched into the professional ranks Thames relied on a very young side by modern standards. The average age of those who played in the first team in that initial season in the Southern League was around twenty-two. Nevertheless, the youthful Irons set about their task with no shortage of confidence.

—co Eight co—

Professionalism and the Southern League 1898/99

The next season they entered the Second Division of the Southern League and won the championship at the first time of asking. The season 1898/99 will also be remembered as the year in which they embraced professionalism. One of the arguments advanced at the time was that none but a tip-top team of good players could draw the multitude to the Memorial Ground. Following its adoption there were more trials and troubles. Those supporters who remained loyal will remember the year as one in which certain officials came under the ban of the FA. It was distinctly unfortunate, and for a time dark clouds threatened the club.

Syd King (1906) in *The Book of Football*

When the Irons took the field at Sheerness for the first game of the season on 1 September 1898 in the Thames & Medway Combination, Sheppey United faced a fully professional team. Arthur Marjeram, the twenty-two-year-old former Aston Villa amateur who had joined Irons from Swanscombe, played at left-back that day. However, the Irons lost their first five games in that competition. A hitch in the fixtures saw Thames playing just one home game in the first six of the season, and this was a friendly, against 1st Coldstream Guards.

Marjeram kept his place for the inaugural Southern League Second Division fixture against Shepherds Bush nine days later. The Irons hit the 'Bush Babies' with three goals without reply on their own turf. Frank Bret, another lad from Swanscombe, was to make his only Southern League appearance for Thames on that historic day. It was also his twenty-first birthday.

The game also marked the debut of Roderick MacEachrane in a Thames shirt. Rod was one of a number of players who Tom Robinson, the Thames trainer, would invite to breakfast with him at his home in Benledi Street, Poplar – a sort of a forerunner of the Cassettari café academy of the 1950s. MacEachrane was one of the club's first professionals and the first player to reach an Irons/Hammers combined appearance tally of 100 games, which he did between 1898 and the end of the 1901/02 season. In all he played 63 games in Thames colours and 60 in the claret and blue of West Ham. Roddy MacEachrane was a creative half-back, scoring 4 goals for Thames and 5 for West Ham. Coming to the capital at the age of twenty, the witty Scot was one of a select band who could lay claim to working in the shipyard (Orchard Yard, Blackwall).

Rod started his footballing career with his local side Inverness Thistle. He was barely five-and-a-half feet tall, but he could tackle hard and his consistency made him a favourite at the Memorial Ground. He was ever-present in the 1898/99 and 1899/1900 seasons and marked the transition to West Ham United with another 100 per cent appearance record in 1900/01. Another fine season in 1901/02, in which he missed only five Southern League outings, caused Woolwich Arsenal to come in for him. At Plumstead he impressed even more than at West Ham and was soon joined by other ex-Hammers, James Bigden and Charlie Satterthwaite.

Rod played an important role in the Gunners' promotion from the Second Division in 1903/04, but major honours eluded him. Whilst he was with them, Arsenal fell at the semi-final stage of the FA Cup in 1906 and 1907. Roddy made his last appearance for Arsenal in the 1913/14 season, just after the club's move to Highbury and the dropping of the Woolwich prefix. He held the record for the highest number of appearances for the club for some years, before his place in the team went to another Scot, Angus McKinnon, who according to an extract from an Arsenal club history by Bernard Joy 'was bigger and more robust but lacking McEachrane's constructive ability'. Roderick passed away in 1952.

The Irons' home debut in the Southern League was a victorious one. Brentford were slaughtered 3-1 on 24 September, with Sam Hay getting a couple – his first and last for Thames. Charlie Dove also got his name on the scoresheet. Hay, from Renfrewshire, Scotland, had joined Thames from Victoria. He was a strongly built inside-right. He had been a regular in the Irons side during their first season at Hermit Road, but he was to get just seven outings in 1898/99.

Chatham were the first visitors in the Thames & Medway Combination on 6 October. This competition and the Southern League both expected their member clubs to field first teams, but the better class of club in the Combination made that the more prestigious target for the Irons.

Back in the Southern League, following a 2-1 defeat at Uxbridge in the next game, the Irons travelled to Wycombe on 29 October and were given a 4-1 hiding in a continuous downpour. As was often to be the case over the next hundred years or so, East London's finest had come to a club that used them to miraculously recover their form. The Buckinghamshire side had lost their previous five matches. Thames arrived at Loakes Park an hour late after missing their train. Jim Aldridge put the Blues two up in the first quarter of an hour and got his hat-trick on the stroke of half-time. Wycombe made it 4-0 before inside forward Jimmy Reid pulled one back for the visitors in the 88th minute. It was to be the Irons' last defeat of the season. The next time the two teams met, at the Memorial Ground on 14 January 1899, Thames were well on their way to the championship. The scoreline was reversed. This time Wycombe had trouble with the transport. Their 'keeper, Ernie Wheeler, missed his connection and arrived at the tail-end of the match. The Bucks boys kicked off with just ten players, with full-back Henry Turner taking up the role between the posts. His career betwixt the sticks didn't get off to the best of starts – one of his own defenders headed the Irons in front. A fan, who was apparently a bit of a regular when Wycombe were shorthanded, was conscripted to defend the visitor's goal. However, this was not going to be a dream come true for him either, as became obvious when he was well beaten by a low shot from Thames centre-half McEwan. David Lloyd spurned two opportunities before grabbing a brace to send the Irons in 4-0 up at the break. Lloyd almost got his hat-trick, sending a penalty wide. Fred Keen scored Wycombe's only goal from the spot. In between the two matches with Wycombe, the versatile Charlie Dove played in every position for Thames.

In the FA Cup, the Royal Engineers Training Battalion had waived home advantage and the Memorial Ground staged an afternoon double bill, staging the tie and an athletics meeting against the Sappers. The Irons met the Royal Engineers three times in 1898/99 and won every game. In the Cup, Thames got through with goals from Gresham and MacEachrane. A crowd of 2,000 people saw them hold Brighton United to a goal-less draw in the next round. Many of these were Irons supporters who had paid the 4s 2d fare to travel from Plaistow to the seaside town. Brighton, from the Southern League First Division, found Moore, Dove and Tranter outstanding for Thames but in the Memorial Ground replay the Irons were outclassed and lost 4-1. This was the last game Alf Hitch was to play for Thames. Wearing the number 5 shirt, he was a particularly fine header of the ball. Hitch was to have just five chances with Thames, but he continued to develop his talents to the extent that he took part in an England trial match two years later. Before becoming committed to football, Hitch, who was from a gypsy family, had been a bare-knuckle boxer and had fought twice for an English Championship. When his days as a player were over he became a gold prospector, firstly in America and then in Australia. It was Down Under that he discovered a good quality jade mine, the sale of which he used to finance a circus, which toured New South Wales during the early part of the twentieth century. By the mid- to late 1920s, he had become one of the pioneer promoters of speedway and it was Hitch who gave the then newsboy Arthur Wilkinson his start in the sport. By 1930 'Bluey' Wilkinson ('Bluey' is an Australianism for a person with red hair) was one of the best riders in Britain – a £100 rider for West Ham Speedway. In later years he would become a World Champion.

By the beginning of 1899, Thames were out of the Cup and had registered only three wins in nine Combination outings. However, in Southern League Second Division they had a 77 per cent success rate. As such, Thames readjusted their sights and priorities and in a spirit of determination they strengthened the squad, starting with the signing of full-back Thomas Dunn from Chatham as the year was turning. Dunn was born in Falkirk in 1872. He had played for the Wolves' 1896 FA Cup final side that was defeated 2-1 by The Wednesday at Crystal Palace. He ran out 13 times for Thames in the last part of their South League Second Division crusade, his first sortie being a 4-0 win at Maidenhead on the final day of 1898. At home in either of the full-back berths, Tom was a consistent starter for the Thames Southern League and Cup campaigns of 1898/99. He returned to the side for the opening match of the following season in a 1-0 defeat at Reading. Dunn donned the number 2 shirt twenty-nine times that season, missing just seven games. Tom left the club before the decision was made to transform into West Ham United and fully embrace professionalism. He was later to return to Scotland and became a successful undertaker.

In February 1899 Warmley, a Bristol side, folded and Francis Payne, the Ironworks secretary, secured the services of three of their leading players. The group included Henderson, who scored 8 goals in his first ten games (the last of the 1898/99 Southern League Second Division season), Peter McManus and George Reid. McManus, a twenty-six-year-old from Edinburgh, was serving a two-week suspension when he signed for the Irons. He had won a Scottish Cup winners medal with Edinburgh St Bernard's in 1895 when they defeated the formidable Renton at Ibrox Park. He broke into the Ironworks team in mid-March 1899, playing in six Thames sides over the following six weeks. He was back in the First XI for the opening game of the 1899/1900 season, but after nine outings up until December 1899, including scoring an FA Cup goal in the first qualifying round against Grays United (his first and last goal for Thames), he was not to figure in the side again. Pete was short for a centre-half, standing just 5ft 7in tall. Previously with West Bromwich Albion, the stocky defender was said to 'play a cautious and waiting game'.

George (Geordie) Reid had formally been with Reading. Geordie was not related to Jimmy Reid, but they played in the same XI for the Berkshire club and took the field for the Irons together in the first five games that George played for Thames. He was most at home at inside-left, but he did play one of his six games for the Irons at centre forward. He scored just one goal in Thames' first Southern League operation, breaching the Southall defence on 25 March 1899 with a shot that knocked the hapless defending 'keeper unconscious as it ricocheted off his head on its way to the back of the net. Geordie went on to play for Middlesbrough in the early 1900s and was in Scotland for the 1906/07 term with Johnstone (Renfrewshire). However, he returned to England to ply his skills with Bradford Park Avenue the following season.

Once Tom Dunn had taken up his place in the Thames defence they did not drop a single point and took the Southern League Second Division championship – their second title in consecutive seasons. The Irons won the final eleven matches in that competition, culminating in a splendid 10-0 win over the bottom club, Maidenhead United. It was rumoured that the future Prime Minister Lloyd George attended the game that day and that this was the start of his lifetime attachment to East London football and to West Ham United in particular. Thames' Combination results also took an upturn and one single defeat in their last seven games enabled Thames to gain a respectable position in that competition. Altogether the Irons went through a period of seventeen successive wins.

However, the secretary still seemed less than a happy man when he responded to the *Thames Ironworks Gazette* at the end of the season.

The only thing needed to make this a success is more support from the men inside the Works. Up to the present we have received very little indeed and can only regret that so many followers of the game prefer to patronise other clubs to the disadvantage of their own. I hope, that next season will see a different state of things.

As outlined above, by this time the club was not the Ironworkers' 'own'. However, this, together with the club's lack of an identifiable fan base in the community, does not fully explain why the Irons failed to attract the support their performances warranted.

Spectatorism

Although he had built the Memorial Ground at great expense, Arnold Hills was, along with others of his class and background, a vociferous opponent of what was then known as spectatorism. The case against the same was put most strongly by the London Playing Fields' Committee, an influential group consisting mostly of ex-public schoolboys committed to extending facilities for playing football and cricket in the Metropolitan area. As the First Report of the London Playing Fields Committee stated in April 1891:

The English love of sport, perverted by want of opportunity for active exercise, produces the gambler and the loafer. Men who, under better conditions, might have developed into active and healthy English people, degenerate into mere spectators at athletic contests, which might almost be compared to gladiatorial shows held by professional giants for the idle amusement of a puny crowd.

Canon Barnett was the founder of Toynbee Hall, the university settlement in Whitechapel. Its youth workers encouraged football in the many clubs founded by the settlement in East London in the late 1800s. Canon Barnett saw the positive aspects of games as forms of rational recreation, but objected to a man 'exciting himself over a match or race where he does not even understand the skill ...' (Barnett and Barnett, 1915). His wife, who agreed with him on most issues, disapproved of 'the football matches, which thousands watch, often ignorant of the science of the game, but captivated by the hope of winning a bet or by the spectacle of brutal conflict' (ibid).

It was Upton Park FC that set the trend for 'spectatorism' in the East London area. Young boys from the large working-class population that built up around the club from the 1870s onwards had the opportunity of seeing the top players of the day in action on their local pitch, where Upton Park played. With no more than a chalk–mark around the perimeter of the pitch, even major FA Cup matches could be viewed free of charge. This probably motivated many boys to take up the game; the spectacle and entertainment these contests offered would have cultivated a taste for watching matches amongst the large numbers of youths and adults attracted to these sporting encounters.

However, old boy clubs, like Upton Park, made up of former public-school boys, had an ambiguous attitude towards those who came to watch matches. In line with the university settlement and the public school mission attitudes, they saw the potential of football as a contribution to improving working-class life and the character development of young men. For the privileged this potential for the betterment of the lower orders lay in playing the game rather than watching it. For all this, however, there were contradictions. Upton Park did not turn away the crowds that came to West Ham Park to cheer them on in their notable FA Cup runs. The historian Mason has noted that even though Upton Park successfully objected to Preston's professionalism following their drawn FA Cup game in 1884, their Corinthian principles did not persuade them to decline their share of the gate receipts paid by the large crowd who had come to watch the match. However, it was perhaps a reassessment of this liberalism and a subsequent realignment with their public school attitudes that led to the final demise of Upton Park.

Following problems with spectators encroaching on to the pitch early in the 1884/85 season, it was reported in the local press (*Stratford Express*, 25 October 1884) that the club's committee was:

... considering whether it will not be advisable to play as many matches as possible on other grounds than their own.

Rather than take such an extreme step, a local supporter wrote to the *Stratford Express* the following week suggesting that the club should have the ground roped off for important matches, as was done elsewhere, but in the end Upton Park decided to play its home matches on an enclosed ground at Wanstead. The club lasted just three more years and was disbanded in 1887.

In line with the prevailing attitudes of exclusivity of his class peers, Hills created The Thames Ironworks Football Club in order that his men could play football rather than watch it. At the same time, football culture in the East End of London and the west of Essex area was not really associated with the Canning Town district, Hills' base of operations. The hotbed of the game in the area incorporated the Forest Gate, Upton Park and East Ham areas. This is where the game was first played in the East End vicinity in an organised manner, and where it was developed in the mid-nineteenth century by the type of men that played for Upton Park FC. Clubs of this kind were to give way to teams made up of local artisans and middle-class players, sides like Barking, Dreadnought, Ivanhoe and Romford. The more professional model of the ambitious Clapton FC followed. In 1887 this enterprising team moved into the Old Spotted Dog Ground in Upton Lane, situated a few hundred yards from Upton Park FC's abandoned pitch. From their first game in September of that year, Clapton began to attract large crowds. Fixtures against the top London amateur teams drew gates of more than 2,000. Contests with professional clubs, like the 1888 encounter with Nottingham Forest, could attract more than 4,000 spectators. Clapton introduced season tickets in 1890 at the cost of four shillings. This gave admission to the club's twenty-four home matches and was accompanied by the promotional information about friendlies against professional clubs like Nottingham Forest, West Bromwich Albion and Notts County at the Spotted Dog.

It is clear that a culture of paying to watch good quality football had been firmly established in the east London/west Essex area by 1890, something that was to continue with Clapton as it established itself as one of the leading amateur clubs in the country over the following twenty years. Thames, and later West Ham, failed to attract significant crowds to the Memorial Ground because there had been no tradition of spectatorism in that vicinity. From 1904 the Hammers succeeded in attracting larger numbers when they moved to East Ham, taking advantage of the tradition of watching top-class football that had been established around that district by Upton Park and carried on by Clapton. Upton Park FC could thus be seen, albeit unwittingly, as having laid the foundations for an appreciation of the quality of football that people would, literally, pay to watch.

From the modern perspective it is hard for us to appreciate that in football, spectators preceded fans and supporters. In the late nineteenth century, football was essentially an athletic event; in its professional incarnation it was close in spirit to the Powder Hall sprint competitions in Scotland and the local athletic events familiar to northern towns and villages. Watching a game was not an end in itself as is the case today. If you were working class you went to a cockfight, a boxing match, a cycling, running, horse or dog race, a dogfight, or a football match. The viewing would be enhanced by the opportunity to speculate on the outcome of competition by way of a wager.

So it can be understood that it was not by accident that the Irons found a temporary home in East Ham and that West Ham United eventually moved from Canning Town to the Boleyn Ground. The club moved to an area attuned to spectatorism and away from the moral imperatives of Arnold Hills, who was against watching football on principle and was appalled by gambling. This ethos that West Ham United moved into is exemplified in the design of the first Boleyn Ground, in particular the character of the old 'chicken run' stand. The design was reminiscent of something between a circus and a racecourse spectator area. Like all buildings, this told its own story. The ancestor of the original working-class motivation to watch sport is still with us. Indeed, 'the pools' now has its own history. But what Ladbrokes and the like offer us in terms of 'football odds' at the ground or in the high street might be seen as the living root of working-class spectatorism.

Thames failed to attract crowds because the club existed in a geographical and moral environment that didn't support the culture of spectatorism that included gambling (the failure of the Browning Road experiment demonstrates the importance of ethical limitations placed on those attending Ironworks games). If it was just success that was needed to attract supporters then the Memorial Ground would have been well attended for much of the time. The fact that this superb stadium never reached half its capacity demonstrates the public school ethic that Hills wanted to inspire, the wish/desire to support the side, to create a sense of loyalty to a name and the ideals associated with that name, had not kicked in. However, interestingly, today that ethic is fully developed in the form of fan loyalty. What we see in the contemporary period as supportership, something steeped in working-class mythology, actually has its roots in the ambitions that a ruling/privileged elite had for those they wished to control/exploit.

Champion Irons

A measure of the Irons' superiority in the Southern League Second Division is indicated in a report of a match in April that noted:

Moore (the goalkeeper) had so little to do that he often left his goal unprotected and played up with the forwards.

The Irons completed their fixtures nine points ahead of their nearest rivals, winning nineteen, drawing one and losing just two of their matches. However, Thames still had to take part in a play-off to decide the title. A little publicised six-club section of the Southern League, representing the South-West, had produced equally decisive champions. Cowes, from the Isle of Wight, had won all their ten games but they could hardly have been pleased when the neutral venue for the play-off turned out to be at Millwall's East Ferry Road ground – 100 miles from the Solent and three from Canning Town. The crowd was nearly all Cockney and thus well pleased when Lloyd put the Irons ahead. Cowes, who had scored fifty-eight goals in their ten League games, pulled one back, but second-half efforts from Henderson and Patrick Leonard gave Thames the victory.

Winger Leonard joined the Irons in 1898. The former Manchester City man scored an impressive eight goals in twelve appearances for Thames, but he caused a sensation when he banged home a hat-trick in his first game for Irons in a friendly against Upton Park. He also scored twice on his second Southern League game, a 4-3 win at Wolverton, which was one of a run of sixteen consecutive victories for the Irons in the Southern League Second Division. Pat hit four in the 10-0 win over Maidenhead in the last match of the season at the Memorial Ground. By the following season he had returned to Manchester City after only five months at Canning Town.

In the end, the play-off was rendered meaningless. Winners and losers qualified for the Test matches. Ironworks were sent to take on Sheppey, who finished twelfth out of thirteen clubs in the First Division of the Southern League. The first match, staged at Chatham, ended in a 1-1 draw: Lloyd scored for the Irons. This was to be the final game that J. Reynolds was to play for Thames. He was a right-winger signed from Gravesend early in the season. Reynolds had scored five goals for the Irons in his previous thirteen appearances for the club. The tricky flanker, who started his career with Leicester Fosse, was somewhat ahead of his time in being able to fire in 'screw-shots' and bend dead balls – much to the consternation of opposing 'keepers. He was never on the losing side whilst with Thames, being in the winning team in all but this, his last game for the Irons.

Before a replay with Sheppey could take place, it was decided to expand the top division and both teams were admitted, along with Queens Park Rangers and Bristol Rovers from outside the League.

It had been another season of glory for Thames. The heady heights of the Southern League now awaited them, but they still had problems. Their biggest crowd of the season had been 4,000 at a 2-0 away win at Southall and there had been two 3,000 gates at the Memorial Ground for the games against Southall and Maidenhead. However, the average Irons home crowd was little more than 1,700. This could not sustain development to the next level, Football League status. Something had to be done – the question was, 'what?'.

—◦ Nine ◦—

The End of the Beginning
1899/1900

The record of 1899-1900, however, would not be complete without some reference to the players who were associated with the club at the time. There was poor Harry Bradshaw, who came from the 'Spurs' with Joyce. How well I remember that match with Queens Park Rangers during the Christmas holidays, when Joyce brought over the sad message to the Memorial Ground that our comrade had passed away. Poor Harry was one of the cleverest wing-forwards I have ever known, and he was immensely popular with everybody. He joined the club with me, and with us in the team were McEachrane (now with the Arsenal), Craig (Notts Forest), my partner at full-back, Carnelly, and Joyce. We had some rare talent in our reserve team too, for, if my memory is not at fault, there were J. Bigden (now of the Arsenal), R. Pudan (Bristol Rovers), and Yenson (Queens Park Rangers).

Syd King (1906) in *The Book of Football*

In the final season of the nineteenth century, the Irons again changed their home strip to red, white and blue, with Cambridge blue shorts. All seemed to be well for the Irons as they looked to reconcile their place in the professional sphere. According to the club secretary, speaking to the *Thames Ironworks Gazette,* 'nothing succeeds like success'. However, beneath the surface, arguments about professionalism continued to simmer. It seemed that the president still had views on this issue. In June 1899, in his article entitled, 'Our Clubs', Arnold Hills disapprovingly told the *Thames Ironworks Gazette*:

But in the development of our clubs, I find another tendency at work which seems to be exceedingly dangerous. The committees of several of our clubs, eager for immediate success, are inclined to reinforce their ranks with mercenaries. In our bands and in our football clubs, I find an increasing number of professionals who do not belong to our community but are paid to represent us in their several capacities.

In some ways the committee running the football club could have seen these comments as complimentary. They were looking to build a competitive football side in order to attract supporters. In his article, Hills was implying that the club should represent the community of the Ironworks and look to find its players and supporters there – but if he believed that, why had he provided a ground that could hold as many as 120,000 people and sponsored the team in the recruitment of players that would enable the club to participate at a level that made professionalism inevitable? Hills went on with some considerable vehemence:

Like the ancient Romans, in their period of decadence, we seem to be willing to be artists and sportsmen by proxy; we hire a team of gladiators and bid them fight our football battles … Now this is a very simple and effective method of producing popular triumphs. It is only a matter of how much we are willing to pay and the weight of our purses can be made the measure of our glory. I have, however, not the smallest intention of entering upon a competition of this kind: I desire that our clubs should be spontaneous and cultivated expressions of our own internal activity; we ought to produce artists and athletes as abundantly and certainly as a carefully tended fruit tree produces fruit.

However, for the committee the 'fruit' was the produce of its team. The club had to choose between being a recreational facility for the Ironworks or becoming a vibrant, professional football club for the East

End and despite these protestations, it was Hills' money that provided the committee with the necessary capital to invest in new players. Among the new signings was full-back E.S. (Syd) King, who, during his long tenure with Thames and West Ham, was perhaps the apotheosis of the transition from amateurism to full professional attitudes and organisation.

Syd King – full-back and apotheosis

King was born in August 1873 in Chatham, Kent. After his education in Watford he went to work in an ordnance depot in his hometown. King started his football career as a full-back with Northfleet, where he claimed to have conceded a hat-trick of own goals for the club in a match against Charlie Paynter's hometown club, Swindon. Paynter was to have a long association with West Ham and King.

Syd was transferred to New Brompton (the club that would become Gillingham FC) in 1897 and spent two seasons in Kent before joining Thames in the summer of 1899, along with team-mate Alec Gentle. At the time, King was thought to be the best full-back in the Southern League. Almost as soon as he signed, Derby made a bid for him.

A bad ankle injury sustained in the encounter with Spurs at the Memorial Ground on 10 March 1899 ruled him out for the rest of the season. King recovered to go on to play for West Ham in 1901. Although he was still formidable as part of a full-back pairing with Charlie Craig and played a total of 89 games for Thames and West Ham between 1899 and 1903, King was never quite the same player again.

Syd was appointed club secretary in 1902, while still playing. His final Southern League appearance was in a 1-1 draw with Kettering, on 15 April 1903, although he did continue to play after this, on occasion in the London and Western Leagues.

It is fascinating to speculate on the possible future for football in East London, had those overtures from Derby in the first days of King's career with Thames been successful. Anything that King achieved in his playing career was destined to be eclipsed by his success as the first manager of West Ham United. King oversaw the move to the Boleyn

Ground in 1904 and the transition to full professionalism and Football League membership in 1919. Through his understanding of the power of the press and skilful manipulation of the media over the years, King, almost single-handedly, introduced West Ham to League Football. With the assistance of Charlie Paynter, who would follow him as manager of West Ham, Syd improved the performance of his side throughout the Hammers' first three League seasons. In one eventful term, 1922/23, he took West Ham to their first Wembley final and broke into the First Division of the Football League. King kept West Ham in the top flight for nine seasons, finishing in sixth place in 1928/27 – a feat not to be equalled for twenty-two years and not bettered until John Lyall led Bonds, Brooking, Lampard and company to fifth place at the end of the 1978/79 season. It could, therefore, be argued that Syd King was the greatest manager ever to reign at Upton Park. Whatever your opinion, Syd, to this day, casts a giant shadow over the Boleyn Ground.

King saw several of the players he worked with develop to international level, but West Ham were relegated at the end of the 1931/32 season. He had let his side grow old. This was evident from looking at the West Ham team beaten at Chelsea in the last First Division game of 1931/32. It included three members of the Wembley side. Although his position was not under threat, King insulted at least one director in a drunken rant during a board meeting to discuss team matters on 7 November 1932. At an emergency board meeting, it was decided that:

Mr King would be suspended for three calendar months from 9 November 1932 without salary and further stipulated that he shall not visit the ground during this period.

After this period, if the directors could be satisfied that his behaviour had improved, it was recorded that he might be reinstated as secretary only and that his salary would be reduced to £8 per week. Yet another meeting of the directors on 3 January 1933, however, decided that King should not be employed in any capacity. The board had also expressed concern about King's honesty in the day-to-day business of running the club. This marked the end for King at West Ham. His ostracism and humiliation were complete.

The new secretary Alan Searles (who was himself sacked for defalcation in 1940) advised King of the decision and informed him of the board's offer of an ex-gratia payment of £3 per week for 'as long as the company sees fit'. But less than a month later, the most successful manager in the history of West Ham United and Thames Ironworks to that point was dead. He imbibed an alcoholic drink laced with corrosive liquid. An inquest jury recorded a verdict that King had taken his own life whilst of unsound mind, after his son had told them that the Hammers' former manager-secretary had been suffering from paranoia. He had been, it was said, 'quite satisfied' with West Ham's offer of a £3 a week 'pension'. A decade earlier the *East Ham Echo* had stated in its FA Cup final issue: 'West Ham is Syd King'. In many ways this is still true. Syd King laid the foundations of what we see now as West Ham United Football Club.

'One-eyed Falco', Garibaldi and 'poaching' Charlie Bunyan

Francis Payne was still not satisfied with the Irons' playing strength and it was his drive to build an even stronger Thames side that was to prove to be his downfall. Payne procured the services of an agent, Charlie Bunyan, to seek out well-known players with a view of bringing them to the Memorial Ground. Canning Town mythology suggests that Bunyan was a relative of one Antonio Falco, known around the district as 'Tony Two-Hats' or 'One-eyed Falco'. Local wisdom has it that Falco, a former employee of Thames Ironworks, although advanced in age, was called on because of his military experience, to help out with and give advice on the training of the Ironworks players before the arrival of Tom Robinson. Falco may have continued to help out in this capacity during Robinson's break in service with the club.

It is not unlikely that Falco would have been an occasional member of the elite Robinson breakfast club at this time, along with Robert

'Fatty' Allan, who made his debut in a 3–1 away defeat at Southampton on 16 December 1899. Allan, who apparently had a great weakness for toffee apples and doughnuts, was one of those who bridged the gap between the works team and the independent club, and went on to appear for West Ham United up to the 1901/02 season. With his single goals for both the Irons and the Hammers, Allan became one of the relatively few players to score for both progenitor and successor clubs. In common with his team-mate and fellow Scot Charlie Craig, Bob hailed from Dundee. Allan's wing-play was to be eulogised in a 1900/01 West Ham handbook:

Shows excellent judgement in everything he does, and can take hard knocks and play on as game as ever. Centres on the run, and occasionally contributes a long shot with plenty of steam behind it. Doesn't neglect his inside man and although weighty, can show a rare turn of speed when necessary.

Antonio Falco was fabled, as a young man living in Caprera, Italy, to be a follower of fellow Italian Giuseppe Garibaldi, famed soldier of the Risorgimento and romantic guerrilla leader. Like Garibaldi, Giuseppe Mazzini, a luminary of Italian nationalism, influenced the teenage Falco. Falco, under the leadership of Garibaldi, took part in an abortive republican uprising in Piedmont in 1834. Threatened with a death sentence, Garibaldi escaped to South America, where he lived from 1836 to 1848, taking part in conflicts in Brazil and assisting Uruguay in its war against Argentina as the commander of its small navy. Later he took charge of an Italian legion at Montevideo that included Falco. Garibaldi shot to international fame thanks to the elder Alexandre Dumas. Dumas eulogised Garibaldi in his writing and the freedom fighter lived up to his image, making public appearances in his vibrant gaucho attire.

Still with the faithful Falco in his train, Garibaldi returned to Italy in April 1848 to fight in its war of independence. His adventures against the Austrians in Milan and his struggle against the French military support of Rome and the Papal States, which divided Italy geographically, made him a national hero in Italy and a figure of renown in Britain, and he was admired in the highest quarters. It was at this time that Antonio began to use football with the men he fought alongside, partly to keep them fighting fit during lulls in the conflict, but also to help them develop an idea of teamwork and tactical awareness. It worked well, making his section one of the most formidable in Garibaldi's command.

For Garibaldi, Papal influence morally and politically dominated the fragmented regions that would one day be the Italian nation. This left them economically stagnant and militarily vulnerable to the ambitions of the likes of the powerful Austro-Hungarian Empire. The bottom line of his philosophy and his dreams of creating an Italian State was that the strength of the people could only lie in the unity of the people.

Defeat in Rome in 1849 left Garibaldi, and Falco as one of his rebel army, with no alternative but to retreat through central Italy. Garibaldi's beautiful, Brazilian wife and fighting comrade Anita died during this period. Eventually Garibaldi was obliged to flee his native shore yet again, first to North Africa, then the United States, and Peru. His men dispersed across the globe, with Falco finding work in the shipyards of East London.

Garibaldi, the 'hero of two worlds', was unable to return to Italy until 1854. In 1859 he helped Piedmont in a new war against Austria, leading a volunteer Alpine force that captured Varese and Como. During May 1860, Garibaldi set out on the greatest venture of his life, the conquest of Sicily and Naples. This time he had no governmental support, but Premier Cavour and King Victor Emmanuel II decided it was unwise to go so far as to challenge the now popular idol of the people. They stood ready to help, but only if he was successful. Sailing from near Genoa on 6 May with 1,000 Redshirts, one of which was Falco, Garibaldi reached Marsala, Sicily, on 11 May and made himself dictator in the name of Victor Emmanuel. In the Battle of Calatafimi, which followed on 30 May, his guerrillas defeated the regular army of the King of Naples. A popular uprising assisted his capture of Palermo. This brilliant victory persuaded Cavour that Garibaldi's volunteer army should now be covertly supported by Piedmont.

Garibaldi crossed the Strait of Messina between 18 and 19 August and in a lightning operation reached Naples on 7 September. He fought the biggest battle of his life on the Volturno River during the first week of October. This was where Antonio lost an eye – the wound ending his fighting days. At the end of the month Garibaldi handed over Sicily and Naples to Victor Emmanuel. Frustrated and affronted by the failure to be installed as Viceroy in Naples, Garibaldi went home to Caprera, situated off of Sardinia. Falco, after over a quarter of a century as loyal disciple, returned to his adopted home and the wife and child he had left near the banks of the River Thames. His injury, together with his propensity to alternate headgear between a flat cap, always worn with the peak pulled down the back of his neck, and the fez-like gaucho chapeau favoured by Garibaldi himself, brought him his local nicknames that probably gave him his place in Canning Town folklore.

Garibaldi continued to be concerned with the capture of the Papal States. In 1862, the Italian government, fearing international repercussions, intercepted him at Aspromonte, where he was wounded in the heel and briefly taken captive. Over the next few years, Garibaldi toured the world looking for support for the cause of a united Italy. In 1864 he came to London where he met with Queen Victoria but also made a semi-anonymous, unofficial visit to the East End to meet with his compatriot Antonio Falco.

Refreshed and encouraged by his travels, Garibaldi led another attack on Rome in 1867. This time he was stopped at Mentana by French troops. However, the world had not heard the last of the man. In the Franco-Prussian War that raged between 1870 and 1871, Garibaldi led a group of volunteers in support of the new French republic. Giuseppe Garibaldi will be remembered for hastening the unification of Italy and for being a leader of genius. A man of the people, he was far more able to motivate the masses than his political contemporary Cavour or mentor Mazzini. As he entered his old age he became politically disenchanted and declared himself a socialist. He died on 2 June 1882.

What happened to Antonio Falco's politics is not known. Maybe there are some clues in his habit of donning the hat he wore throughout his campaigns with Garibaldi and in the embryonic Thames Ironworks FC calling on him in the winter of his days. Perhaps he had picked up some of Garibaldi's ability to engender a marshal spirit and meld disparate forces to a focus on a mutual end; what philosopher David Hume saw as the definition of art, the ability to bring heterogeneous elements into an homogenous whole, which might be seen as the feat that characterised the Italian game in the last third of the twentieth century.

History turns to legend, and legend fades into the mists of myth. The flame of Falco's life was kept flickering by word of mouth and the few people that have heard the faint echo of his existence, illuminated by his small but significant activity in the shadow of two giants, Giuseppe Garibaldi in the past and West Ham United in the future.

Charlie Bunyan had been a professional footballer and had kept goal for Hyde FC in an FA Cup-tie against Preston North End. In that game he let 26 goals slip past him, making any subsequent accusations about the veracity of goalkeepers pale into insignificance. Whilst in pursuit of his duties for Thames, Bunyan had missed an appointment with a player in Birmingham. Not wanting to come away empty-handed, the nothing-if-not-time-efficient Bunyan approached another player unannounced and unsolicited. However, 'walls have ears', and Birmingham had its share of Football Association 'moles'. Charlie was subsequently deemed to have been indulging in the nefarious act of poaching and he was summoned to appear before an FA disciplinary panel. Following investigations, it came to light that Francis Payne had financed Bunyan's efforts to lure players to Canning Town and the club secretary was judged to have misused a large sum of money (rumoured to be as much as £1,000) which had been given to the club by Arnold Hills.

The FA suspended Charlie Bunyan for two years. Payne failed to attend the FA hearing into the matter and was suspended until he did appear. In addition, the club was suspended for two weeks from 1 September and fined £25. Shortly after the FA ruling, Payne announced that he had resigned as secretary of Thames Ironworks Football Club at the close of the previous season. One can only speculate on the embarrassment and shame this affair brought to the door of the Corinthian-spirited president of Thames Ironworks Football Club, Arnold Hills. All his worst fears about what he saw as the cancer of professionalism must have seemed to be encroaching on his vision of what his football club should be.

George Neill, who had played his last game for the club only six months earlier, became the club's third secretary. Neill was then twenty-five and, during his term in office, he continued the now traditional strengthening of the playing staff, particularly prior to the start of the 1899/1900 season. Sadly, Neill died at the tragically young age of thirty.

Charlie Bunyan was never to return to English football. Maybe resuscitating his family links, he was rumoured to have gained employment within the evolving game in Italy. Over a decade later it was believed that it was he who had been instrumental in arranging the legendary unofficial London Ladies' visit to Rome, who were skippered by Plaistow-born Nelly Paynter – thought to be a cousin of Charlie Paynter, the West Ham manager from 1932 to 1950. The story was that this competition, a series of three test matches against Rome Ladies, took place around 1910. Sir Thomas Lipton, the famous tea merchant, allegedly sponsored it. Most of the young women that made up the London side were recruited in the East London area. Indeed, it is believed that the team did play in claret and blue and were going to carry the name of West Ham until it was decided that it would create greater interest if the tourists were understood to be a London XI. Whilst there are no substantiated records, the tale of the series tells of how the first match was abandoned because of torrential rain and was declared a draw. The second game ended with the two sides sharing 10 goals. London won the final game 7-3. The goalscorers included Alice Amelia Stanton and Maria Anita Falco, granddaughters of 'Tony Two-Hats', the Italian freedom fighter Antonio Falco. Although playing in goal, Nelly also scored, from the penalty spot.

London Ladies were thus proclaimed European Champions and should have played a Uruguayan side the following year to contest the World Championship, but for unknown reasons this never happened.

The European Ladies Cup was brought back to England by the team's manager, former Arsenal and Thames Ironworks captain, Bob Stevenson. The trophy was supposed to have been kept in the original Boleyn Castle, but it seems to have disappeared when the building fell into disuse some decades before the structure was demolished in 1955. Nelly never returned to East London. Anecdote informs that she struck up a romance with the manager of the famed Italian team Juventus and although there was some twenty years between their ages, the couple married. Their seven sons all played professional football in Italy. Two daughters continued Nelly's pioneering work in women's football, helping to export the female game to the USA following their emigration to New York.

Building, building, building

As much heartache as the poaching scandal must have caused Arnold Hills, the committee of Thames Ironworks were not going to let this inhibit them. Before the start of the season the side was further bolstered by the arrival of Albert Carnelly, a much-travelled forward from Bristol City. At the same time three Tottenham Hotspur players were brought to the Memorial Ground in something of a transfer coup, masterminded by Irons secretary George Neill. The trio were Henry (also known as 'Tom' or 'Harry') Bradshaw, Bill Joyce and Kenny McKay.

Bradshaw, a winger from Liverpool, was to play a dozen games for Thames and he scored his two goals for the club in cup games. Born on 24 August 1873, he joined Thames in 1899 and made his debut against Reading on 16 September.

Tom started his footballing career with Northwich Victoria and was a regular member of Liverpool's Second Division championship-winning teams of 1894 and 1896. On two occasions he was selected to play for the Football League and he won an England cap against Ireland in February 1897. Joining Spurs in May 1898, Tom made his debut and scored against the Irons in a Thames & Medway League fixture.

Virtually an ever-present in the Tottenham side during their 1898/99 campaign, Tom was chosen to represent the United League against the Thames & Medway League. He was also selected for the South *v.* North annual international trial match and he went on to play for an England XI against a Scotland XI in a match to benefit the players' union. After 69 appearances in all competitions for Spurs that season, he transferred to Thames in the summer of 1899.

The highlight of Tom's all-too-short Irons career was destined to be his four goals in an 11-1 Thames & Medway Combination thrashing of Grays United. Tom, like the man who signed him, was dead before he had reached the age of thirty: he died at the age of twenty-six on Christmas Day 1899 of consumption. Bradshaw was a key figure in terms of the future for Thames and his death, attributed to an injury received in a match against Bedminster the previous October, stunned the club.

Bradshaw was a courageous, fast and direct left-winger. He played and scored in the 2-1 FA Cup defeat at the hands of Millwall just sixteen days before his death in front of a record 13,000 crowd at the Memorial Ground.

Spurs and Thames met on 2 April 1900 in a match to raise funds for Bradshaw's dependants. Frank Taylor, the youngest player ever to play for Thames' Southern League team, took over the left-wing spot from Bradshaw. Tipped by the writer of the club's handbook to become 'one of the finest outside-lefts in the kingdom', the former Harwich man served the Irons and West Ham from 1889 to 1902, taking the field for Thames 28 times and scoring 6 goals. Unfortunately, he never realised the level of notoriety predicted for him at the start of his career.

The 1899/1900 campaign was to be the only season that Bill Joyce, a centre forward typical of the Victorian age, was to play in the Southern League in Thames colours, but in his 35 appearances he netted on a commendable 18 occasions. Joyce began his career with Greenock Morton in his native Scotland before transferring to Bolton Wanderers in 1894, where he sustained a broken leg in 1896. He had also been a prolific marksman for Tottenham, scoring 26 times in 38 appearances in a Spurs shirt.

Bill left Thames for Portsmouth as a replacement for Sandy Brown, who had ironically moved to Spurs. A year later he found himself turning out for Burton United, where he played for another two seasons, appearing in 29 matches.

Inside forward Ken McKay, in his only season with the Irons, was to appear 36 times on the team sheet and 13 times on the score sheet. Ken won an 1897/98 First Division championship medal in his season with Sheffield United. His transfer to Spurs for the following season was something of a surprise for Blades supporters, but he made a scoring debut for Tottenham – sadly at the expense of Thames – on 3 September 1898. Bill Joyce benefited greatly from McKay's presence at both Northumberland Park and the Memorial Ground. Ken laid on many scoring opportunities for the big centre forward, most of which he took the fullest advantage of. Ken moved to Fulham in July 1900. He helped the Cottagers to win the Second Division of the Southern League in 1901/02. McKay scored in his first matches of three different competitions for Spurs, but had to wait until his second outing for the Irons before scoring twice in a 4-0 victory over Chatham on 18 September 1900 at the Memorial Ground.

The make-up of the Irons was to cause some disquiet amongst Thames' Southern League First Division opponents. For example, when the Irons travelled to Reading on 16 September for their first game in the upper heights of the Southern League, immediately after their FA suspension had been lifted, Thames were greeted with some criticism.

The *Reading Standard* commented cynically that the Thames team lining up for the first game in the Southern League First Division 'had a familiar look about them' and that 'anybody can get up a good team with plenty of "ready" behind them'.

Reading won 1-0, but two days later the Memorial saw McKay and inside forward Carnelly grab two goals each in a 4-0 win over Chatham. This was followed by a Memorial Ground win over Bedminster. Things started to gel and there was a feeling that the Irons were going on to repeat their feats of the previous season at the higher level. Four FA Cup games had produced 21 goals, including the seven that were smashed past the Dartford defence. This was the start of Dundee man Charlie Craig's career with Thames. Craig, at thirty-six, was one of the older troopers in the Thames ranks. A member of the last Thames side and the first West Ham team, he was involved with both from 1899 to 1902. The tall Scottish full-back became one of East London's most popular players, making a combined total of 102 appearances for Thames and West Ham. He began his career in earnest with Our Boys, in Dundee. He played half a dozen matches and was promoted to the first team, which ultimately combined with the East End club to become Dundee FC. Charlie originally moved south to work as a mechanic at Tate Sugar Refinery at Silvertown and then Thames Ironworks, but with the toleration of professionalism, football became Charlie's main occupation and he tried a number of positions before settling his 6ft 1in, 13st frame at left-back. One of the last links with the old Ironworks club was severed when he joined Nottingham Forest in the Football League.

Described by a writer of the time as being a 'genial, good-natured giant', Craig was also a keen athlete and won a host of medals for his achievements on the track. He left Forest for Bradford Park Avenue, then moved on to Norwich City in 1908, but he returned to Bradford PA at the end of the 1908/09 season. Sadly, yet poetically, Charlie passed away on the same day in 1933 as his former full-back partner and Hammers manager, Syd King.

As has often been the way of football in East London, hopes were raised only to be dashed. In the next match, in early November, the Irons conceded seven goals at a muddy White Hart Lane.

Bouncing back from the Tottenham disaster, the Irons hammered Grays United 11-1 in the Thames & Medway Combination with Bradshaw and Carnelly each netting four. However, fortune continued to be mixed in the Southern League. Three points out of four were picked up at the Memorial Ground against New Brompton and Swindon Town, but a run of seven defeats started with a 2-0 loss at Bristol City. This was Fred Corbett's last game of a total of 3 for Thames. However, he was to become a leading light in West Ham United's first season and he continued to be a vital source of goals during the 1902/03 term. His best display was in a rearranged game against Wellingborough Town on 30 September 1901, after the first fixture was abandoned because of poor light due to the late arrival of the Northamptonshire club. Hammers won 4–2, with Fred scoring a hat-trick. Described as strong and determined, he later had successful spells with Bristol Rovers, Bristol City and Brentford.

Struggle and volume investment

The game against Wellingborough saw H.S. Sunderland take over in goal from Tommy Moore; it was the only game Tom missed that season in Cup and League. Sunderland had previously been with Gravesend United and Millwall and he played 12 Southern League games with the Lions in 1898/99. His nerves must have shown in this, his first and last, game at the Memorial Ground. Sunderland was one of a dozen players – 58 per cent of the 25 starters in the Southern League games – who failed to reach double figures in terms of appearances in that competition during the 1898/99 season. In their championship year, Thames had played 30 individuals with 18 of them (60 per cent) making less than 10 appearances. The consistency of selection is one of the main differences between the modern game and its Victorian ancestor. For example, in West Ham's successful 1963/64 side, 21 players were used in First Division games and only 6 (just over 28 per cent) of these appeared less than ten times that season. John Lyall's West Ham side that finished in the highest-ever spot attained by a Hammers team used only 16 players, of which just 3 (under 19 per cent) failed to make double figures. This shows the impact of modern training methods and physiotherapy, but it also says something about how the economics of the game has changed.

Team squads in the early days of professional football were like regiments in number and organisation. The FA Cup and Southern League competitions were only the tip of the iceberg. Clubs like West Ham in the early part of the twentieth century would play in a range of leagues and cup competitions, fought out between national, regional and local opposition, using first and second teams, 'A', 'B' and sometimes 'C' squads. Later, youth and colt teams would also be involved. These competitions, that have been long forgotten, their details lost in the mists of time, drew big crowds – often on a par with the leagues and cups that we see as important from our modern vantage point, having counterparts in today's game. Wages were relatively low, but employment was high. There was a First World War mentality about the way players were used and a gladiatorial ethos within the game. The physical nature of the football in those days saw players cut down in their prime on mass, in swaths. There were five players waiting to take the place of every man that limped from the field of play after the 90 minutes – not during as there were no substitutes – and no quarter was given. One played on with the effect of exacerbating injury, rather than stopping to alleviate it.

With the coming of the modern era, clubs began to invest in particular talent, nurturing individual players. Like the infantry soldier of today the contemporary footballer is a highly trained professional, well equipped and supported by vast technical back-up, but in the early days skill and ability were exploited in a much more general way. Many young men went like lambs to the slaughter. Now investment in players is concentrated, it is rationalised in the same way as most modern production methods. In the time of Thames Ironworks Football Club and later the adolescent West Ham United, however, the investment was in volume – a high turn-out, high-input strategy.

Irons hang on

The defeat by the Lions in the FA Cup denied Thames a place in the hat with the Football League clubs. It was around this time that wing-half W. Stewart, who had been signed from Luton, made his debut for the Irons. It was the thirteenth game of the season, on 13 January 1900, in a 1-0 Memorial Ground defeat by Reading. He played his first sixteen matches of the season as skipper, but it is perhaps not surprising that he didn't reappear in 1900/01 when the records show that Thames only had five wins under his leadership.

By mid-season, it was clear that the Irons were finding life difficult in such exalted company as Millwall, Spurs and Southampton. With only three games left they had won just three times in fifteen outings. When Thames met Southampton at the Memorial Ground, a mere twelve days before the Saints were due to contest the FA Cup final at Crystal Palace against Bury, it was clear that the Irons really needed to win all their remaining matches to avoid the threat of relegation. Perhaps Southampton were conserving their energy, but Thames won 4-1. The hero of the match was Bill Joyce, who scored a hat-trick and was carried from the field by Thames supporters grateful for two badly needed points. Jubilation was cut short, however, when, the very next day, Cowes and Brighton United announced their resignation from the Southern League and the East Londoners were left exposed at the foot of the table with Sheppey United. If Thames gained maximum points from their remaining games then they could possibly overhaul both Chatham and Gravesend and claw their way to safety.

The Irons did indeed win both games, but so did Chatham and Gravesend. Thames finished bottom of the table, having won only 8 of their 28 games. This obliged the club to contest a test match for the second successive season. Unlike the previous season, the Irons were looking to preserve rather than better their status. Fulham were the side looking to usurp Thames' place. The Cottagers were Southern League Second Division runners-up by the narrowest of margins from Chesham and Wolverton. The match took place at Tottenham. Former Thames forward David Lloyd was now a Fulham player, one of only six survivors from the previous meeting between the clubs; Thames had won that game 1-0. A mighty charge in the first half saw the Irons go in at the break four up. This allowed Thames to play out a much more measured game in the second period. Just 600 people saw the 5-1 victory over the West Londoners. On his return to his old Spurs stamping ground Bill Joyce conjured up yet another crucial hat-trick.

Thames were safe for another season, but the fact remained that the Memorial was unable to attract sufficient numbers to match rising expenses. By 1900 the club were pulling in new players from professional clubs from every part of Great Britain. This meant that they had no option but to increase ticket prices. The committee swung its weight behind an aggressive ticket-selling campaign, using the *Thames Ironworks Gazette* and local newspapers. In the last two years of the nineteenth century, season ticket prices doubled from five shillings to 10 shillings. The committee did attempt to minimise any resentment about this inflation by introducing, for the first time, concessions for 'ladies' – 5/6 (tickets in the grandstand only) – and a 3/6 price for 'boys', but gate receipts were still insufficient. It was clear that the club was still (and whilst they persevered at the Memorial Ground would be) reliant upon the finances of Arnold Hills. However, the Thames president remained unhappy about the committee's increasingly professional outlook and behind this was the limit to his generosity and his lack of willingness to continue to invest in a project with no financial or productive return. A crisis was brewing, and something would soon have to give.

~ Ten ~

Frank Clarke Hills

Will you that claim resist
Ye men of Canning Town?
The song is seldom missed
Until the bird has flown;
Will ye withhold support?
'Tis all their leaders ask,
Your men have "held the fort"
Proved equal to the task,
Assist to make the outlook brighter,
'Twill make Lew Bowen's heart feel lighter.

From *May West Ham still remain United* by AC – Cricket Rhymester

The Greenwich Chemical Works

In 1804, on the east-side area on the Thames Peninsula which became the Riverway area of Deptford and in 2000 was to become the site of the Millennium Festival, soap maker George Russell built a large tide-mill over the site of an artesian well.

The first organised association football games played to common regulations were taking place within the sound of a blast of a big ship's hooters, not too long after George Russell built his mill to the east of Greenwich Marsh. It was designed on an industrial scale and used to grind corn. During its construction the boiler of a steam engine, designed by steam pioneer Richard Trevithick, exploded. This accident was to become famous in the history of steam engine development as it exposed innate deficiencies in the technology of the time, changing the way steam power was to develop.

In 1840, six years before Charles Mare watched his *Mosquito* glide into the waters of the Thames, Russell's mill, by then known as the East Greenwich Tidemill, came into the hands of Frank Clarke Hills as part of the settlement of his marriage to Ellen Rawlings. The large site had excellent wharfage facilities, ideal for a business that depended on water transport. Under the ownership of Hills it is probable that corn continued to be ground at East Greenwich. From 1845 it was described as 'a steam flourmill' – the tide mill having been replaced by a 25-horsepower steam engine.

On the riverbank to the north of the mill, Frank Hills erected a chemical works. This was gradually extended. In the 1840s, housing was built for the chemical works employees near the mill in Riverway. It was called River Terrace and added to the existing Ceylon Place built at the same time as the mill (parts of Russell's 'New East Greenwich' housing and a public house, 'The Pilot Who Weathered the Storm', that was named in honour of William Pitt, can still be seen). There was a big house on the riverside, Frank Hills' foreman's house. This is where the works manager Thomas Davies and his family lived. Today, the Greenwich Yacht Club's clubhouse stands on the site.

The smell of the chemical works, which was of 'an acid and sickening character', caused widespread complaint in Greenwich, and Charlton and annoyed the garrison at Woolwich, which was three miles away. One of the works' operations might conjure up something of the impact of this stink. It manufactured manure from shoddy, which was a concoction made from waste leather, dry bones, bone ash and refuse from sugar bakers – in short, whatever organic rubbish could be bought cheaply, piled up and mixed with sulphuric acid. The toxic fumes of manufacture took its toll on the workforce, with some dying from the effects. In 1871, Mr Pink, the Medical Officer of Health for Greenwich gave advice designed for 'abatement of the nuisance which these works could scarcely have failed to occasion'.

Victorian entrepreneur and industrial innovator

Frank Hills, owner of the F.C. Hills & Co. Chemical Works, was an industrial chemist, who hitherto had been based in Deptford. He was an almost perfect example of the Victorian businessman. His chemical works at East Greenwich grew consistently over fifty-year period and, with his brothers, he developed a model of early industrial capitalist development, controlling a range of linked commercial manufacturing and production concerns that amounted to an expansive empire stretching from East London to Spain, from Wales to South America.

Frank Hills has a rather opaque lineage. His father, Thomas, appears to have moved to Bromley-by-Bow just before 1810. At the start of the nineteenth century, Bromley-by-Bow was a busy industrial area that boasted the largest alcohol industry in the country. It was a district of mills, mostly driven by the tides of the River Lea, but not the Bromley Steam Mill, the mill that Thomas Hills had taken over from C. & J. Millward in 1811. Thomas used the mill for grinding corn and the manufacture of chemicals, converting the waste materials from the early gas industry. What he manufactured is unknown, but his accounts show that he used considerable quantities of this material between 1824 and 1827, indicating that the Bromley Steam Mill was chiefly a chemical company during this period.

An account of Thomas's activity was written in 1827, about the time when he seems to have left Bromley-by-Bow, possibly because of bankruptcy. This places his factory in Bromley, Kent. This inaccuracy has been replicated elsewhere, but as the St Leonards, Bromley Rate Books testify, Thomas Hills lived in Bromley-by-Bow. A letter also exists, written in careful large letters on squared paper, which confirms this. It was addressed to Bromley Steam Mills and is from Thomas's son Frank, who would have been about eight when he wrote it in 1815.

The Hills ancestry seems to have been Kentish. It was in this county, in Kemsing, in 1700 that a Richard Hills of Underriver rented a field to a William Wells. The families of Wells and Hills had a long history in Penshurst. The Wells family were shipbuilders, industrialists and politicians. However, it is uncertain what Thomas Hills had done or where he had resided before his arrival at Bromley-by-Bow, although there is an appreciable amount of circumstantial evidence that places him in Somerset. Thomas married a Sara Clarke; her surname had been associated with the district of Lyme for hundreds of years. Thomas junior, having been named after his father, was probably their eldest son; he was born in Lyme Regis in 1804. Another, son, Henry, married Charlotte, who was from Lyme. In the eighteenth century Lyme was a holiday resort and a naval seaport, but it also had a relatively large chemical industry and was also the source of the clay used for Coade stone, the terracotta used throughout London, the mixture of which was said to be a secret. Lyme may well have been where Thomas senior learnt the skills of industrial chemistry.

Thomas Hills and Uriah Haddock identified an innovative process for the manufacture of acid and took a patent out for this in 1818. It was revolutionary and chemists and industrialists came to Bromley to see how it was done. The discovery is described in almost every history of the chemical industry and this illustrates its importance in the development of the manufacturing and production in this area. It was not long before Thomas was obliged to go to law following infringement of patent by Thompson and Hill of Liverpool. Defending inventions and procedures related to the chemical and gas industries was a practice that his son was to become adept at. In two or three cases, Frank fought legal battles that dragged on for decades. A proportion of this legal action appeared to be less justified than it might have been, but he seemed to have made a good deal of money out of these proceedings through compensation and contract settlements. For example, an appeal from a consortium of gas companies that went to the Privy Council showed that Frank Hills had 'received £107,377 0s 9d in royalties. His expenses rated £16,942 ... and ... £6,450 for his own salary after paying the same sum to his brother, Thomas, and some large sums to other brothers ...'. This was a time when top gas executives and engineers could expect a salary of around £1,000 per annum. As such, it can be seen that Frank Hills had an astute business instinct. He was involved in an almost endless process of developing and exploiting partnerships with other innovators.

Early in the 1830s, Frank Hills began to contact the London gas companies from the Deptford Chemical Works that he rented from Frederick Beneke. Beneke, who came from a family with a strong background in chemistry and metallurgy, lived in Denmark Hill, in Camberwell, not too far from Frank who resided in the same district, in North Terrace. In 1836 the London & Greenwich Railway was built across Deptford Creek, and included a gas works alongside the line on a site next to Deptford Chemical Works. It was said that when the gas works became independent of the railway, Frank provided a mortgage on it and it was in this gas works that he experimented on gas industry waste. He carried out a great deal of research at Deptford, continuously experimenting in the laboratories and the engineering workshops chiefly focusing on gasworks wastes. His collaborators at this time include the mysterious Reverend Dale and a German chemist by the name of Mr Baufe. Whilst testing the impurities of a batch of guano, he discovered a means of extracting iodine. This was an important breakthrough and the firm went on to undertake this industrially. Sulphur was also refined at Deptford and sold to Kentish hop growers.

By the mid-1830s, several London gas companies were using Frank Hills' methods and in the early 1840s the Hills' business expanded to include a short-lived chemical works at Battersea and could have been involved with the Hills Chemical Works in Wandsworth, which failed and was subsumed into Wandsworth Gas Works.

Frank Hills did not confine his business interests to the chemical industry. In the early 1840s he became known for the development of steam road vehicles. The best-known promoter of steam road vehicles was Stratford-based Walter Handcock. During 1839, Frank travelled on a Hancock vehicle on a trip to Cambridge, as a contemporary engineering journal was to relate, 'taking a lesson on steam carriage construction during the journey'. He later patented a gearing system that Fletcher in *Steam Locomotion on Common Roads* suggested had originally been developed by Roberts of Manchester. His work on steam cars appears to have been undertaken in collaboration with the General Steam Carriage Co. of East Greenwich. Some well-publicised trips were taken over particularly steep and difficult hills in the area, but the venture seems to have been unsuccessful. Sixty years later his son, Arnold Hills, was to take up road-vehicle manufacture.

The Hills brothers won prizes for their innovations in the chemical industry at the 1851 Great Exhibition, with some of the products of gaining worldwide recognition. This included material he exported to the West Indies to be used in the sugar cane industry.

The profits of the chemical industry appear to have been invested in heavy engineering. In 1871, at a time when he was at his peak of activity with the gas companies, Frank acquired a controlling interest in the Thames Ironworks & Shipbuilding Company.

Perhaps prophetically, this was the same year the FA Cup competition was introduced. It was to help bring the game to a wider geographical constituency and promote an understanding of the rules throughout England and beyond. Former Upton Park player A. Stairs was at the meeting that came up with the idea and was on the sub-committee that chose the trophy. His in-depth knowledge of the rules of the game was such that he was invited to referee the first three FA Cup finals.

Clubs were emerging with unprecedented speed in the Midlands and North. Whilst a number of these new clubs were the product of the activity of ex-public schoolboys, many of those who later joined their ranks were artisans, tradesmen and factory workers – a substantial number of these men proved to have a talent for the game. The growing leisure industry, which developed alongside industrial manufacturing, offered these individuals the chance of supplementing their earnings by playing in front of paying spectators, and not a few took up the opportunity. Some were sufficiently skilful to take up the game on a full-time basis. It is certainly true that well before professional football was legalised in 1885, many clubs had made payments to players to turn out for them.

Just as Frank Hills was a pioneer within his industry, this was the beginning of what would become commercial football. It was the start of the laying of the necessary foundations for development. To understand football as an enterprise it has to be located in its beginnings in the industrial development of the first mature capitalist economy, Britain.

In the last third of the nineteenth century, the Thames Ironworks & Shipbuilding Company was thought to be the greatest shipyard of all. Frank Hills was to be Chairman of the Board of this great enterprise until his death in 1895. However, Frank had been involved with the Thames Ironworks as a member of the Board sometime before 1864, first appearing on the list of members for a new shares issue. It is likely that he had an interest from the time that Thames Ironworks had been established following the bankruptcy of C.J. Mare in 1856, when the company had been launched with a capital of £100,000 in £5,000 shares, all sold on the first day of issue to local engineering companies.

Frank's involvement with Thames Ironworks paralleled the company's golden age. By the early 1870s, the firm led in its field in every conceivable way. The peak of this period occurred in the 1890s when they specialised in quality work. The impetus from this era of excellence carried them, alone on the Thames, into the twentieth century.

Frank relished his role as Chairman of Thames Ironworks. Tales about his enthusiasm abounded. He explored each new battleship with all the excitement of a boy as, in the embrace of the Thames, it kissed the waves for the first time. He had no way of comprehending that he was living through the final phase of shipbuilding on London's river. He could not have guessed that it was his son's destiny to struggle in vain with the Government and preside over the closure of his yards and the loss of the skills that had made them renowned on the face of the planet.

The Forgotten Giant

In the parish church of St Luke, in Chiddingstone Causeway, Kent, you will find a memorial to Frank Clarke Hills. Like a good number of London-based industrial entrepreneurs who scaled the heights of success on the banks of the river, Frank retired to the Kent countryside. He spent his final years at his home, Redleaf, on the hill above Penshurst Place with his zoophytes and a new gramophone. To his last days he could recite *Paradise Lost* in its entirety, knowing it by heart. In the last years of the twentieth century the only parts of this once grand and beautiful structure were the gateposts and lodge. Designed by J.C. Loudon, a leading garden architect of the time, the posts had been commissioned by William Wells, the shipbuilder, the owner of Redleaf before Frank acquired it, squaring a 300-year circle between the Hills and Wells families. When Frank Hills came to live at Redleaf in the 1880s, like Wells, he was also a father to battleships.

When Frank Hills died in May 1895, reports of his death were restricted to two or three lines in local newspapers. It took until 29 July for *The Times* to publish a report of his will, which had been lifted from the *Illustrated London News*. It had been discovered that this practically anonymous South-East London chemical manufacturer had left a personal fortune of £1,942,836 11s 1d. When W.D. Rubenstein analysed the wealth of the Victorian era in 1977, he showed that just forty individuals in the period between 1809 and 1914 left more than £2m. Frank Hills was very close to being included in this exulted company. Between 1880 and 1899, sixty-nine British millionaires had passed on – just three chemical manufacturers can be found amongst the names. As such, Frank Hills can be recognised as a giant in his field and there is no evidence to suggest that he inherited huge wealth. His brother, Thomas, who died in comfortable circumstances, left just £3,657; another brother left £20,909. His passing was closely followed by the death of his two eldest sons. Even from the grave Frank was still 'at it'. It took three years from the day he died to discover that the buildings and site of his main factory were not his and had to be removed from his estate. However, this only amounted to a value of £1,583.

Frank Hills was a great Victorian industrialist – probably a genius – but remains almost unknown. There is a document in the Kent County Archive that details Frank's agreement to hand power of attorney to his sons. It is signed in a feeble hand, his butler acting as a witness. The Deptford Chemical Works was put into the hands of Thomas Herbert Hills, the son of his departed brother, Thomas. The husbands of Frank's two daughters, Constance and Annie, administered the company from a distance. Within a few years the organisation that Frank Hills had founded and nurtured was bankrupt. The works at East Greenwich was taken over by the South Metropolitan Gas Company and George Russell's mill was converted to a power station. South Met had taken over most of the South London gas works during the 1870s and were one of the biggest concerns in the British gas industry by the last decade of the nineteenth century. During the First World War, they were to use part of the site for research into chemical weapons.

Frank Hills filled a gap in gas industry, doing the seemingly impossible, making a huge amount of money from its vile and noxious waste products. This was a man who followed the lineage of Merlin and the mystic path of the medieval apothecary. Guided by a sexton of the rough science that evoked the Victorian nightmares of Frankenstein's monster and Jekyll and Hyde, he fulfilled the ancient dream of alchemy. In the bubbling, steaming, acidic atmosphere of the laboratory he turned base metal into gold. He exploited his own intelligence and the wisdom of others, being willing to learn from those around him and work hard on his enthusiasms. He rode roughshod over the patent system to mercilessly exploit the potential of his industry. His success blossomed out of his ingenuity, doggedness, and his energetic and seemingly boundless enthusiasm. He left gas company directors exhausted and exasperated. He left competitors gasping in his wake. However, he remains more or less unremembered by general history and uncelebrated by his industry.

—⁂ Eleven ⁂—

The Hills Boys

Go! travel if you will
Great Britain round and round,
O'er valley, dale, and hill,
Where battlefields abound,
You will find on your way
Spots hallowed and renowned
But none to bear the palm away
From your Memorial Ground,
'Tis there in future years we ought
To see the English Final fought.

From *May West Ham still remain United* by AC – Cricket Rhymester

Frank Hills was only one prominent member of an energetic family. There were several brothers, sons, daughters and nephews. Between them they achieved enormous success, stretching the bounds of their own family empire and pushing the parameters of their industrial context. As a phenomenon they represent a model of capitalist development in transition. The development of their informal consortium was very much based on a family nexus, but it was set in the secular and rational environment of commercial enterprise. It is unlikely that we will ever see their like again, but their example stands as an historical monument to them as a vibrant family and as creative individuals, and also to their dynamic era.

Four brothers, a sister, a nephew and an uncle

Thomas Hills was the eldest brother of Frank Hills. Thomas, who was later to patent a boiler grate, was looking for a job in 1846, so he applied for the post of Deputy Superintendent at the Phoenix Gas Works in Greenwich. He said that he was 'a good practical chemist and accustomed to the control of workmen' and would want a salary of £300 a year. Phoenix turned him down because he was too experienced. After that he worked for his brother, Frank, dealing with the commercial business at the works, both at Deptford and East Greenwich. In the early 1870s he joined Frank on the Board of Thames Ironworks.

As an old man Thomas lived at 8, The Grove, on Blackheath with his second wife and their young son, Thomas Herbert, who was described in 1891 as a 'student of chemistry'. It was he who inherited the Deptford Chemical Works. Thomas's four daughters, the eldest in her mid-thirties, were still living with him in the 1880s. He died in 1885.

Another brother, George, seems to have worked for Frank at Deptford. He held joint patents with Frank and gave his address as the Deptford Chemical Works. George appears to have been active in dealing with these patents, because the record says that he 'swore in Chancery'. This indicates that he was involved in the sugar industry. George was still alive when Frank made his will in 1890, but although Frank left money to all his other brothers he left nothing directly to George, choosing instead to bequest a sum to be used for his benefit. That seems to imply that George was not able to make his own decisions and perhaps he needed to be cared for.

Arthur Hills gave his address as Norwood when he witnessed Frank's marriage agreement in 1847. It may be that he managed the chemical works, which the family owned at Nine Elms and, perhaps, another in Wandsworth. In the 1850s, Arthur owned a chemical works on the Isle of Dogs at Millwall, immediately across the river from East Greenwich called the Anglesey Works. It was in an area known as Folly Wall – where in the 1990s a housing complex was built. He also rented a plot of land at Deptford Creek next to the Deptford Chemical Works for nearly thirty years. He appears to have passed away around 1891, as he was alive when Frank made his will in 1890, but dead before Frank died.

Henry, who was younger than Thomas and Arthur, having been born after the family moved to Bromley-by-Bow, spent much of his life commuting between Anglesey in North Wales and South London, where he lived in one of the high-quality dwellings in Blackheath Paragon. His chemical works were situated in the odd industrial village of Amlwch, on the northern tip of Anglesey (suggesting a link with the chemical works on the Isle of Dogs). It can be concluded that Henry probably lived part-time in Anglesey because he had a farm not far from his chemical works and several of his many children were born there.

Henry seems to have moved to Almwych in 1840 and he established a fertiliser factory at Llam Carw, on the exposed headland overlooking the tiny harbour. It is now an open cliff top where walkers enjoy sea views and only the clinker of Henry's works remains underfoot. The Anglesey works closed in the 1890s.

There is some vague indication that Henry might have some connections with Birmingham since his eldest child, Alice, was born in Edgebaston in the late 1830s. In 1859, *The Times* recorded a partnership in a Bromsgrove salt works involving a Henry Hills. Salt production is not so very far removed from some of the chemical manufacture that the Hills family was involved in. In 1863 there is evidence of a Hills sister, Jane, when Henry acted as executor to her will.

The Hills family also had interests in the field of mineral extraction. Above Almwych stands Parys Mountain, from which copper has been extracted for hundreds of years in a breathtaking landscape. About a mile to the west of the Parys Mine at Morfa Dhu, Messrs Hills and Sons of Almwych worked a bluestone mine. This material was broken down into copper, lead, zinc, silver and other elements in smaller proportions. This is the only mine clearly identified as belonging to the Hills family, but they seem to have interest in other mines.

D.C. Davies managed a phosphate mine at Berwyn in North Wales on behalf of Frank Hills and its product may have been used at Almwych. Davies worked the mine between 1872 and 1884, but it does not seem to have been successful. D.C. Davis could well have been related to Thomas Davies, the Greenwich Chemical Works manager. Both men were from Oswestry and were of about the same age. Thomas Davies had a family of four daughters who produced a lively and interesting family magazine, much of it dealing with their holidays in Anglesey.

Frank Hills also owned the Ponderosa copper mine in Huelva, Spain from 1876. The area is now within the Rio Tinto area. In 1889 he acquired the Buitron Mines and in 1891 the Buitron and Huelva Co.'s assets included a railway line. This meant that the family controlled the Buitron, Zalonea, Ponderosa and Conception copper mines. United Alkali took over these Spanish mines in due course.

In 1860 Henry made agreement with the Mona Mine Company. He became active in the small business community in Almwych and was elected to the harbour board, perhaps reflecting his company's reliance on shipping. Harbour records relating to Henry's firm show shipments of raw materials from Spain and Antwerp. In 1889, the fiftieth anniversary of the chemical works in Amlwch was marked in these records together with details of its products.

At some time before 1897, Henry Hills had taken over a former smelting works complex on another harbour. This is now the site of a housing estate.

It is likely that the Hills family owned other foreign concerns apart from their mining interests. Letters exist which indicate considerable travel abroad on business by Frank. The company certainly imported South American guano into Deptford where it was refined.

Henry and Frank probably co-operated with each other in business. Henry ended his days described as a chemist of Dartford, although the Anglesey business was clearly still thriving. Like Thomas he became a member of the Thames Ironworks Board in the 1870s. He died in 1897 at 6, Northbrook Road, Lee – a smaller and rather less fashionable address than the Paragon. He left a son, Charles Henry, who was to fulfil an important role in the family business. He seems to have had a home in Tynemouth, although he too appears to have spent much of his time in Blackheath and died in Bromley, Kent. In Newcastle he managed the Low Walker copper works. It was called the Anglesey Copper Company and was sited on the Tyne with a smelter at Low Walker.

Edward Septimus Hills of Newcastle had some connection with the Anglesey works. He died in Hendon, North London in the 1880s. His brother, James, had a son, also by the name of James, who was a printer in Sunderland. The gas company minute books sometimes record a J. Hills. This could be another brother who kept the Newcastle end of the business going before Charles Henry went there. If there was also a James, then Edward Septimus could well have been Thomas senior's seventh child.

The Newcastle works is likely to have smelted copper extracted from the family mine in Spain. It would not have made sense to bring the same material from Anglesey, which could have been dealt with by the existing smelter on site there. The common name given to the works in Newcastle and Millwall, 'Anglesey', suggests that some of the by-products of copper smelting were used in London.

The Hills brothers' uncle, Robert, who was probably a City of London-based merchant, had connections with South American metal mining, maybe having visited that part of the world himself, which, in the first part of the nineteenth century was full of European fortune hunters. The Hills family had a continuing interest in metal mining and they also had enough capital to buy a substantial property in the 1820s. This may have been a family link with the Mexican copper mines. Many years later South American guano was used by Frank Hills at Deptford, and Thames Ironworks built vessels to aid in the exploitation of this material.

Magnificent diversity

None of the owners of Thames Ironworks restricted the company to shipbuilding alone. Its civil engineering projects included major roof building – for example, at Fenchurch Street Station – and at one point the firm put in a futuristic design for Wembley Stadium. Under Peter Rolt, Thames Ironworks fabricated the iron for the International Exhibition Building in South Kensington, the Royal Aquarium, Westminster and Alexandra Palace in the north of London. During Charles Mare's time, Thames Ironworks forged the ironwork for Blackfriars, Hammersmith and Westminster Bridges, the North London Railway Bridge and sections of the rail bridge over the Menai Strait. Other bridge building included the Saltash and the Britannia tubular bridges. Under the stewardship of Arnold Hills, Thames Ironworks built the new 'Iron Bridge' in 1896. Anyone who has ever approached Newham from Tower Hamlets in the west will know this piece of engineering that effectively links Canning Town and Blackwall Tunnel, crossing the river Lea. It straddled the old boundary between Middlesex in the west and Essex to the east. The gradient of bridge it replaced always posed a problem to certain types of traffic, but the steep incline and awkward bends of the new structure were still an obstacle to horse-drawn vehicles in 1902. This was when a deputation of Silvertown traders pressurised West Ham Council to attend to the problem, and improvements were eventually made – in 1929. The new 'Iron Bridge' was replaced with a larger steel structure in 1932. Thames Ironworks produced all its own iron and steel for these projects. The latest twenty-first century development builds on these foundations.

The company took over the Greenwich engine builders John Penn and Sons in 1902 and parts of Penn's works were given over to producing a range of cars and lorries. It was this expansion that led to the manufacture of road vehicles at Greenwich and Vauxhall. There were several models, one of which, a coach, can be seen today at Beaulieu Motor Museum. Another was powered by a 60 horsepower, six-cylinder engine. It broke all speed records from 50 to 300 miles, reaching over 75 miles per hour. A 12 horsepower vehicle saw service as a London taxi. The firm had workshops at the famous motor-racing track Brooklands, and used the circuit to test car components. In 1911, almost as a final hooray, Thames Ironworks produced the dock gates for HM Dockyard at Devonport.

It is probable that Frank Hills and his family were involved with many more enterprises than are detailed here. It has recently come to light, for example, that Frank Hills had a large site on Stratford High Street. Stratford had a large concentration of chemical works. This interest was sold to a soap company.

A dynamic heritage

This chapter gives a picture of the diversity and energy of the Hills family throughout the Victorian era. It also provides an idea of another part of the context out of which Thames Ironworks Football Club arose. The club that was to become West Ham United had as its seed the commercial and entrepreneurial forces of the most pulsating period in history. Its forefathers were energetic, industrious innovators, willing to take risks and looking to extend boundaries and fight in the face of all odds to achieve their ambitions, part of which was to be the best. This is part of the institutional culture of what Thames Ironworks was. Like all the other influences that this book has analysed, the forces that shaped and moulded the football club could not be resisted or repressed. What the Hills family understood is that organisations must develop or die.

And then they were Hammers

Your favourites still maintain
Their quenchless dash and go,
When did their courage wane
Against their worthiest foe?
Then welcome theme renew,
Repeat the chorus loud and long,
Cling to the old 'Light Blue',
Whate'er in future may betide them
As staunch supporters stand beside them.

From *May West Ham still remain United* by AC – Cricket Rhymester

As Ironworks fade, Hammers appear

In the last months of the nineteenth century it seems that Arnold Hills finally realised that a club with a broad enthusiastic following might not be compatible with amateurism, and he began the slow process of drawing back from the logical consequences of the situation that he had created. This was evident in a piece he wrote for the *Thames*

Ironworks Gazette during this period, which seemed at the same time to be proposing a kind of compromise:

The clubs of ours have to grow, but let them always represent our own people. It may be necessary, at the beginning, to introduce a little ferment of professional experience to leven the heavy lump; but even then let these professional experts come into the yards to work as well as play.

This idea, a mixture of naivety and shamateurism, was the concoction of a defeated and out-of-touch man whom time and events had passed by. Hills' problem, from his perspective, was that he had created a monster, but the logic of capitalist enterprise was at work and was about to offer him a way out.

Late in the nineteenth century the Ironworks bought out John Penn and Sons and, in order to raise new capital, Hills made his firm a public company. He had issued 4,000 ten-shilling shares, anticipating that they would be undersubscribed. He had offered to buy one share for every share purchased. Shares were offered first to staff at the Ironworks and then to the general public, but there was no rush to buy. At that time the typical working man in the East End would have been hard pressed to find the money for even a single share.

However, eventually Hills was to find himself, for the first time, accountable to shareholders. He was no longer able to act in philanthropic ways as the whim took him. One of the first things that became clear was that the Ironworks could no longer retain their football club. From the new perspective of the public limited company, the Irons and the Memorial Ground represented a burdensome, money-losing operation which was only justifiable if it created better conditions in the Ironworks. Hills no longer believed that its primary purpose was recreation for his workers, nor did he feel that the club contributed to company morale. Hills was still in a position to influence events, but what should he do? He could have done nothing and watched the company abolish the club. His other alternative was to transform Thames and create some initiative by which the continued existence of the team could benefit the Ironworks. He was undoubtedly emotionally involved. Thames had not turned out as he had wanted, but it was his creation; if it disappeared, he ran the risk of this being seen as his failure. There was also the problem of the Memorial Ground. Like the Thames Ironworks Football Club, its most salient characteristic was that it was there. If the Memorial Ground was not used it would stand as silent testimony to the demise of Hills' dreams to create a morally better society through sport, and a football team with whom the local community could identify.

The next move that Hills made was a blend of capitalist inspiration, last-gasp philanthropy and good old British compromise. He kept the team in existence, but severed its formal connections with the Ironworks. He proposed a limited company, but did not use the situation to cut his personal losses and run. He became a major shareholder, urged fellow businessmen and workers to invest in the club and provided the Memorial Ground on very favourable terms (rent free for three years). It was in fact a brilliant solution, but it made him a hypocrite. He had pulled in money from the sale of shares in his football club and made himself a sizable investor in an organisation devoted to making its financial supporters a profit from professional sport.

The Hills family's involvement with the club has endured. Patrick Hills, (Arnold Hills' grandson) is alive and well today. He served in the Navy as an officer in the last war. His cousin, Charles Warner, is one of the directors of West Ham United.

At the end of June 1900, the Thames Ironworks Football Club resigned from the Southern League and was wound up. Within days, the club was reformed under the name of West Ham United and was elected to take the place of the Ironworks in the Southern League. A new secretary, Swansea-born Lew M. Bowen, a clerk at the Ironworks and one-time match reporter for the *Thames Ironworks Gazette,* was appointed. Lazzeleur Johnson, a clerk who lived in Forest Gate, was the first chairman of the board. He worked for Thames Ironworks and had been connected with its Football Club. He purchased ten shares of West Ham United in July 1900 when they were first issued to the public.

One of the first things to change was the team strip. There are a number of theories why the Hammers adopted claret and blue −

most claim some relationship with Arnold Hills, the azure element supposedly tying in with the cobalt of the Old Harrovians or perhaps his representation of Oxford University. However, it is unlikely that Hills would have approved of the besmirching of his beloved amateur ties with the taint of professionalism. It is much more likely that the new colours were adopted partly to provide the new club with a fresh identity and partly in order that West Ham United might be associated with the success of Aston Villa, the club that had won the 1899/1900 Football League First Division championship and three of the previous four League titles. Apart from the characteristic Hammers badge, West Ham's first strip was an exact replica of that worn by the 'Villains' of that period. Packaging and promotion were primary considerations from the very first moments of professionalism. Allegiances to Dagenham Motors, BAC Windows and Dr Martens have been mere contemporary expansions on a basic theme.

Events at Canning Town in the summer of 1900 could not be regarded entirely as a parting of the ways. The new club and the shipbuilders maintained a relationship, albeit an uneasy one, for some years afterwards. However, West Ham United Football Club was registered as a company on 5 July 1900 and Thames Ironworks Football Club passed into history.

'Our extremity is God's opportunity ...'

Arnold Hills joined the Thames Ironworks and Shipping Company in 1880. When Frank Hills died, his third son, Arnold, oversaw the firm as it reached the very pinnacle of its development, between 1897 and 1902. However, when West Ham United came into being there were only 3,100 men working for the Ironworks, just starting to fight a losing battle against yards on the Clyde and in the North of England. Twenty years after the completion of the *Warrior,* the Thames yards were gradually starved of Ministry of Defence orders. Arnold Hills was obliged to make an ever-increasing effort to keep his business viable. The slow decline saw Orchard Place evacuated in 1903.

Through Parliamentary contacts, Hills found out that northern syndicates on the Clyde and Tyne had been formed. This meant that they were able to keep production costs to a minimum and grab new orders from the Ministry. In response, Hills threatened to raise awkward questions in Parliament about the lack of orders his yard was receiving from the Government, the works having received only £1 million worth of orders out of an Admiralty budget of £67 million. It was at this point in 1910 that the Navy commissioned Thames Ironworks to build their biggest-ever dreadnought. At 22,500 tons, this would be the largest and probably the most technically advanced battleship to sail the seas in the history of the world. The board were forced to pull the tender down to foolish levels, but HMS *Thunderer* was launched in February 1911. She was fitted out with her main armament, powerful 13in guns, at the company's works at Dagenham. She was the first ship to be fitted with directional gunfire equipment. However, the project incurred a tremendous financial loss and this, together with the First Lord of the Admiralty, Winston Churchill's refusal to give any further orders to Thames, led to the banks foreclosing on the Ironwork's debts.

The Thames Ironworks' decline was, to a significant extent, due to its heavy reliance on building warships for the Admiralty, which increasingly patronized the less expensive northern yards. Despite the respite provided by the construction of dreadnoughts after the launch of the *Thunderer,* Thames Ironworks came to an ignominious end.

Hills' physical health mirrored his company's degeneration. By 1910 he was arriving at the Ironworks in an invalid carriage; soon after he had become completely paralysed, but he fought to the bitter end, having to suffer humiliation and the constant threat of defeat. Paralysed from the neck down and supported in a specially made invalid basket, he addressed mass rallies in Trafalgar Square arguing for the continuation of contracts for the building of warships in London shipyards. For all this, on 21 December 1912, a notice was pinned to Thames Ironworks' main gate. It read:

Our extremity is God's opportunity and I do not doubt there is still in store for us a Happy New Year.

Not too long after this, Arnold Hills passed away. As a man tied to the fate of his company, perhaps he was always going to 'go down with his ship'. A plaque dedicated to the memory of Arnold Hills can be found on the stairway in Canning Town Station, built in 2000.

The Thames Ironworks & Shipbuilding Company closed just two years before the First World War. If it had survived up to the outbreak of hostilities, this would have ensured its future, and perhaps the survival of large-scale shipbuilding on the Thames, at least into the 1920s, giving the firm a chance to diversify. However, London's river lost its last major shipping concern at the height of the greatest naval shipbuilding boom Britain had ever had. The Great Eastern Railway later took over the Thames premises, but that also failed. Like the ill-fated *Albion*, which after serving in the Middle East during the First World War was sold for scrap in December 1919, Thames Ironworks had served its purpose and was consigned to local memory, becoming another fragment of Britain's industrial archaeology.

Ironically, on the other side of the river, George Russell's tide mill lasted a bit longer. It had been converted to a power station and this was replaced by a more modern structure in 1947. This had become defunct by the 1980s and was demolished, wiping out the last trace of the Hills family on the Thames. One wonders what Frank Hills would have made of it all. Would he have continued building ships on the Thames? Would he have bothered with a football club? The answer to both questions is probably 'no'. Importantly, Frank seemed to understand when to move on. He was an innovator, a man driven by instinct and great energy. His third son, Arnold, was a public school boy through and through. He was motivated and, in terms of his entrepreneurial activity, limited by his ideals and beliefs. Perhaps nothing illustrates the difference between Frank and Arnold more clearly than family stories of how, after Frank's death, Arnold poured a cellar of prize claret down the drain. Arnold, talented, honest, brave and idealistic, ultimately failed. Frank, a master of the cut and thrust, a Victorian genius, made the money.

Arnold Hills had not been let down by his workforce at Thames Ironworks that he, for so long, saw as a threat. If Hills was betrayed, it was by members of his own class – Churchill, the government who had asked him to overstretch his resources to the point of no return and the capitalists of the north who had undercut his production costs by exploiting their workers. For all this, it is probably more accurate to say that Hills was overtaken by the direction of industrial development in shipbuilding. In effect his East London yard had been used as a laboratory, to explore what was possible on the Thames – at the centre of transport, government and commerce. In the end, the contribution Hills and Thames Ironworks made was to push ship production in this context to its limits, maybe represented in the *Albion* and the *Thunderer*. Thames Ironworks showed the world what could be done and shipbuilding went on from there. This was not without cost. Hills, his workforce and a significant proportion of the community that surrounded the Ironworks were chewed up by the grinding of the wheels of shipbuilding commerce.

In December 1990, West Ham Football Club was reunited with the Royal Navy after a gap of eighty-six years. A glass copper painting charting West Ham's football history and its connection with Thames Ironworks was commissioned by West Ham United and was presented to Captain Allen of *HMS Warrior* at Portsmouth. If you ever look at this painting, perhaps as you watch the next match that West Ham play, you might give a thought to those who started it all, the people who made it all possible – the founding fathers of the Irons: C.J. Mare, Frank and Arnold Hills, Charles Dove, the hardworking Ted Harsent, Dave Taylor, and the unlucky Francis Payne. But most of all, remember those whose final view of this world was the launch of a great ship, the *Albion,* and the men who built her with the ceaseless 'clank' and 'thunk' of the West Ham riveting hammers.

Statistics

1895/96

All home games played at Hermit Road

Club secretary: *A.T. (Ted) Harsent*
Captain: *Robert Stevenson*
Highest attendance: *3,000 v. Chatham (a), FA Cup 1st qualifying round, 12 October 1895*
Biggest win: *8-0 v. Manor Park (a)*
Biggest defeat: *6-0 v. Millwall (a), friendly, 14 December 1895*

41 friendly matches
1 FA Cup match
5 West Ham Charity Cup matches

1896/97

All home games played at Hermit Road

Club secretary: *Francis Payne*
Captain: *Robert Stevenson*
Biggest win: *4-0 v. Marcians (a), London Senior Cup, 7 November 1896*
Biggest defeat: *8-0 v. Sheppey United (a), FA Cup 1st qualifying round,*
    10 October 1896

12 London League matches
1 FA Cup match
2 West Ham Charity Cup matches
7 London Senior Cup matches
1 Essex Senior Cup match

London League Table

	P	W	D	L	F	A	Pts
3rd Grenadier Guards	12	9	1	2	32	13	19
Thames Ironworks	12	7	2	3	17	17	16
Barking Woodville	12	6	3	3	20	11	15
Ilford	12	7	1	4	26	14	15
Crouch End	12	4	2	6	14	19	10
Vampires	12	3	1	8	10	28	7
London Welsh	12	0	2	10	9	26	2

The Scots guards withdrew during the season and their record was deleted. London Welsh were suspended near the end of the season and as a result Thames Ironworks were awarded two wins.

1897/98

All home games played at the Memorial Ground

Club secretary: *Francis Payne*
Captain: *Walter Tranter*
Biggest win: *7-3 v. Bromley (h), London League, 15 January 1898*
Biggest defeat: *3-1 v. Ilford (h), London Senior Cup, 22 January 1898*

16 London League Cup matches
3 FA Cup matches
3 London Senior Cup matches

London League Table

	P	W	D	L	F	A	Pts
Thames Ironworks	16	12	3	1	47	15	27
Brentford	16	12	2	2	43	17	26
Leyton	16	8	4	4	41	33	20
3rd Grenadier Guards	16	7	3	6	34	33	17
Ilford	16	5	7	4	33	25	17
Stanley	16	5	4	7	22	22	14
Barking Woodville	16	2	6	8	16	37	10
Bromley	16	4	2	10	20	49	10
2nd Grenadier Guards	16	0	3	13	17	42	3

1898/99

Club secretary: *George Neill*

Captain: *Walter Tranter*

Top scorer: *David Lloyd, 14*

Highest attendance: *4,000 v. Southall (a), Southern League Second Division, 4 March 1899*

Biggest win: *10-1 v. Maindenhead (h), Southern League Second Division, 15 April 1899*

Biggest defeat: *4-1 v. Brighton United (a), FA Cup 2nd qualifying round replay, 19 October; 4-1 v. Wycombe Wanderers (a), Southern League Second Division, 29 October*

22 Southern League Second Division matches

3 FA Cup matches

1 championship decider

1 Test match

Southern League Second Division Table

	P	W	D	L	F	A	Pts
Thames Ironworks	22	19	1	2	64	16	39
Wolverton	22	13	4	5	88	43	30
Watford	22	14	2	6	62	35	30
Brentford	22	11	3	8	59	39	25
Wycombe Wanderers	22	10	2	10	55	57	22
Southall	22	11	0	11	44	55	22
Chesham	22	9	2	11	45	62	20
St Albans	22	8	3	11	45	59	19
Shepherds Bush	22	7	3	12	37	53	17
Fulham	22	6	4	12	36	44	16
Uxbridge	22	7	2	13	29	48	16
Maidenhead	22	3	2	17	33	86	8

1899/1900

Club secretary: *George Neil*

Captain: *Tom Bradshaw*

Top scorer: *Bill Joyce, 15*

Highest attendance: *13,000 v. Millwall Athletic, 9 December 1899*

Biggest win: *7-0 v. Dartford (a), FA Cup 3rd qualifying round, 28 October 1899*

Biggest defeat: *7-0 v. Tottenham Hotspur (a), 4 November 1899*

28 Southern League First Division matches

7 FA Cup matches

1 Test match

Southern League First Division Table

	P	W	D	L	F	A	Pts
Tottenham Hotspur	28	20	4	4	67	26	44
Portsmouth	28	20	1	7	58	27	41
Southampton	28	17	1	10	70	33	35
Reading	28	15	2	11	41	28	32
Swindon Town	28	15	2	11	50	42	32
Bedminster	28	13	2	13	44	45	28
Millwall Athletic	28	12	3	13	36	37	27
Queens Park Rangers	28	12	2	14	49	57	26
Bristol City	28	9	7	12	43	47	25
Bristol Rovers	28	11	3	14	46	55	25
New Brompton	28	9	6	13	39	49	24
Gravesend United	28	10	4	14	38	58	24
Chatham	28	10	3	15	38	58	23
Thames Ironworks	28	8	5	15	30	45	21
Sheppy United	28	3	7	18	24	66	13

Bibliography

Barnett, Cannon, S.A. and Barnett, H.A.(1915) *Practicable Socialism,* London: Longman, Green

Belton, B. (1997) *Bubbles, Hammers and Dreams,* Derby: Breedon Books

Belton, B. (1999) *Days of Iron,* Derby: Breedon Books

Belton, B. (1998) *The First and Last Englishmen,* Derby: Breedon Books

Blows, K. and Hogg, T. (2000) *West Ham. The Essential History,* Swindon: Headline.

Fishman, W.J. (2001) *East End 1888,* London: Hanbury

Green, G. (1953) *The History of the Football Association,* London: The Naldrett Press

Hogg, T. and McDonald, T. (1995) *1895-1995 Hammers 100 Years of Football,*
    Independent UK Sports Publications

Hogg, T. and McDonald, T. (1995) *West Ham United Who's Who,*
    London: Independent UK Sports Publications

Kerrigan, C (1999) *Upton Park F.C. 1866-1887: gentlemen footballers in West Ham Park,* in *Rising
East: The Journal of East London Studies,* London: Lawrence and Wishart

Korr, C. (1986) *West Ham United,* London: Duckworth

Lovesey, P. (1970) *The Official Centenary History of the Amateur Athletic Association,*
    London: Guinness Superlatives

Mason, T. (1980) *Association Football and English Society 1863-1915,* Brighton: Harvester Press

Mills, M.(1999) *The Early East London Gas Industry and Its Waste Products,* London: M.Wright

Moynihan, J. (1984) *The West Ham Story,* London: Arthur Baker Ltd

Northcutt, J. and Shoesmith, R. (1993) *West Ham United. A Complete Record,* Derby: Breedon
Books.

Northcutt, J. and Shoesmith, R. (1994) *West Ham United. An Illustrated History,*
    Derby: Breedon Books

East and West Ham Gazette, 10 November 1888

Stratford Express, 25 October 1884

Stratford Express, 1 November 1884

Stratford Express, 17 September 1890

Ward, A. (1999) *West Ham United 1895-1999,* London:Octopus

Wigglesworth, N. (1996) *The Evolution of English Sport,* London: Frank Cass

Printed in Great Britain
by Amazon